CHRISTIAN BELIEF
AND THIS WORLD

CHRISTIAN BELIEF
AND
THIS WORLD

The Firth Lectures
in the
University of Nottingham
1955

ALEC R. VIDLER

SCM PRESS LTD
56 BLOOMSBURY STREET
LONDON

First published in Great Britain 1956

W5032

200029649

Printed in Great Britain by
The Camelot Press Ltd., London and Southampton

Contents

Preface

An earlier and shorter version of these Firth Memorial Lectures was delivered on the Sir D. Owen Evans Foundation at University College, Aberystwyth. I am grateful to the responsible authorities both at Nottingham and at Aberystwyth, first, for inviting me to lecture and, then, for allowing me to deal with the same subject and, most of all, for the exceedingly generous way in which they received and entertained me.

A. R. V.

The Cloisters
  Windsor Castle

Introduction

I asked to be allowed to lecture on 'Christian belief and this world' because it is a subject that has been exercising my own mind for many years, and it is desirable that a lecturer should be keenly interested in his subject, even if nobody else is. But I know from personal experience that my interest in the subject is widely shared. A great deal has been written about it, not least in our own time, but I believe it needs much more exploration and clarification than it has yet received. If this book goes any way towards meeting that need, it will be largely due to the fact that over the years I have had the opportunity of picking a good many other people's brains. Whatever readers may think of the argument of Chapters I to IV, I am confident that they will be grateful to me for having brought to light in Chapters V and VI some of the wisdom that lies hidden in the files of *The Christian News-Letter*.

By 'this world' in the title of the book I mean both *this* world as distinguished from any other worlds that may exist, and also the *world* in the sense of civil society and the political order as distinguished from the church or ecclesiastical polity. But that will become clear enough as we proceed. As regards what I mean by 'Christian belief', I shall naturally have much to say about that too, directly and indirectly. The complaint is often and (in my opinion) justly made that theologians and Christian spokesmen as a whole, when they talk or write about Christianity, do not start far enough back and that they take too much for granted. Perhaps therefore I may be allowed to say that this book is a kind of sequel to a book entitled *Christian Belief*,[1] which contained a course of lectures that had been delivered in Cambridge University. I am neither so presumptuous nor so immodest as to suppose that readers of this book

[1] Published in 1950 by the S.C.M. Press.

should be expected to have read that. I allude to it only because if anyone should desire an ampler explanation of what I mean by 'Christian belief', which does start from the beginning, it is available there.

For everyone who takes Christianity seriously, few questions can be more important than what Christians ought to believe about this world and what their practical attitude to it ought to be, and by way of introduction I will call just two witnesses to corroborate my own estimate of its importance, one living and one dead.

Professor Amos Wilder of Harvard has recently said that 'the one great and telling charge made against the Christian religion in the modern period is that it is otherworldly, escapist and irrelevant to the problems of this life'.[1] He has also said that the charge of false otherworldliness 'is responsible for the apostasy from Christianity of extensive groups and strata today'.[2]

The question whether Christians may or may not value what this world offers is certainly one by which many thoughtful people are genuinely puzzled. Some do not hesitate to say, what a university professor said in my hearing a short time ago, that if Christians really practised what they preached they would have to go in for complete world-renunciation. Indeed, my second witness, the late Bishop Gore, writing in 1926, went so far as to say: 'In the last year or two I seem to have become more conscious how large a part of the prevalent refusal of hearty belief in Christ by thoughtful people is due to the idea that his claim for world-renunciation is hopelessly extreme.'[3]

I need not, however, enlarge this introduction, because the whole of the first chapter is intended to bring out as sharply as possible the two sides of the main question with which the book is concerned.

[1] A. N. Wilder, *Otherworldliness and the New Testament* (1956), p. 7; cp. *ibid.*, pp. 18 f.
[2] A. N. Wilder, *Eschatology and Ethics in the Teaching of Jesus* (1950), p. 70.
[3] C. Gore, *Can we then believe?*, p. 188.

I

Should Christians be Nonconformists?

'WHOSO would be a man must be a nonconformist', remarked Emerson sententiously. It is no wonder that someone said of him that he was born in a pulpit! Emerson was not using the word 'nonconformist' to mean one who refuses to conform to an established church. He meant by a nonconformist what we should call an individualist: the sentence I have quoted comes from his essay on 'Self-Reliance'. I am not myself going to use the word in either of those senses. I am not going to ask whether Christians should refuse to conform to an established church—interesting as that question may be. Nor am I going to ask whether Christians should be individualists or self-reliant. What I am going to ask is whether Christians should be nonconformists vis-à-vis *the world*. Albert Schweitzer speaks somewhere of 'living in genuine nonconformity to the world',[1] and we might say that he has done so himself. Is that what all Christians ought to do? 'Do not be conformed to this world', says the Apostle.[2] Are we meant to take that injunction literally, or may we tone it down or explain it away,—or anyhow what do we make of it? That is the question.

[1] A. Schweitzer, *Christianity and Religions of the World*, p. 85.
[2] Rom. 12.2.

Here is a case in point taken from real life—the case of a well-known historical figure and a famous statesman upon whose conscience the problem of what to do about this world always pressed heavily. The enigmas in the personality and in the career of Mr Gladstone are, I would say, due to the fact that throughout his life he was intensely aware both of the call not to be conformed to this world and of the necessity of being conformed to it or at least of dealing with it on its own terms. 'All his life,' as Sir Philip Magnus says, 'he did his best to reconcile a nineteenth-century political career with the Gospel and example of his Saviour.'[1]

It was my job for about ten years at Hawarden in North Wales to look after Mr Gladstone's library which he bequeathed to the nation. I used often to think what an extraordinary man he was. He was one of those powerful personalities who combined so many physical, intellectual, moral and spiritual gifts that he was bound to go to the top whatever career he had followed. If he had become a lawyer, he would have been Lord Chancellor. If he had become a clergyman, he would have been Archbishop of Canterbury. As it was, he went into parliament, and inevitably became prime minister. But what struck me most about Mr Gladstone was that he lived a double life. He was not only a great statesman, a man of action tirelessly engaged in national and international politics. He was also a man of thought, almost a recluse with the dispositions of a monk and an immense zest for learning and the cultivation of the spiritual life.

This comes out in the way he divided his time. In those days parliament sat for only about six months of the year. During those six months Mr Gladstone lived in London, absorbed in political affairs, moving freely about in society, engaged in the interests of the world. During the other six months he lived at Hawarden Castle, in rural retirement. Leaving politics behind, he spent long hours in his study, known as 'The

[1] Philip Magnus, *Gladstone,* p. 110.

Temple of Peace', reading and writing books and articles on classical, literary and theological subjects, brooding on the mysteries of human existence, communing with the God in whom he so fervently believed. At Hawarden he lived an ascetic life, getting up at six in the morning, daily attending the morning service in the village church, and observing strict hours of study and contemplation.

Not only did Mr Gladstone live this double life of conformity and nonconformity, but there was a constant conflict between the two going on in his own soul. That is why he seemed again and again to be on the brink of retiring from politics in order that he might without distraction devote himself to the life of the spirit. But each time the pull of political responsibility and of the exercise of power in the affairs of the world proved stronger. He was still presiding over the government of his country when he was well over eighty, and he finally resigned only because of failing physique.

As a young man he had very seriously considered devoting his life directly to the service of the church and, even after he had abandoned the idea of taking holy orders, he attempted to form a lay brotherhood. It is tempting to speculate what the result would have been if the pull of nonconformity had proved stronger than that of conformity. At all events, it is easy to imagine that in another age and in other circumstances he might have become the founder of a great religious order like St Dominic or Ignatius Loyola or the moving spirit in a religious revival like John Wesley. Indeed, as it was, his life-long work for the redemption of prostitutes carries him into the company of such men as General Booth. No work could have been more nonconformist than that or more scandalous from a worldly point of view, and it is not surprising that his political friends anxiously urged him to abandon it.

One of the familiar enigmas of Mr Gladstone's career may be partly explicable by the consideration that the ecclesiastical nonconformists enthusiastically followed this high anglican as their political leader because they perceived that, in a sense more important than the ecclesiastical, he *was* a nonconformist —a nonconformist to the world.

The case of Mr Gladstone shows how this problem of conformity or nonconformity can weigh upon a man's life as well as upon his thought and press it in opposite directions. Ought Christians, guided and supported by their faith, to engage in the manifold activities of the world in which they have to live, seeking to influence the course of its history and looking for tangible results? Or ought they to be detached from the world and to expect nothing from it, looking always to that other city which is said to have everlasting foundations? A variety of answers has been given to this question by Christian thinkers down the centuries. Dr Richard Niebuhr in his book *Christ and Culture* distinguished five different types of answer, and later I shall have occasion to mention what they were.

But at this stage I am going to state the two sides of the problem as simply and as starkly as possible. So, first, here is the case for Christians' being nonconformists to the world and for their being as detached as possible from its interests and its ambitions.

II

The foremost thing to notice is that thorough-going nonconformity seems to be plainly prescribed in the New Testament, and that the first Christians made no more attempt to cut a figure in the affairs of this world than their Master had done. Does not that set the true standard for all Christians?

Jesus Christ said that his kingdom was not of this world, and in the New Testament he and his followers are represented as being in a state of deadly enmity with it. He told his disciples that they must forsake all that they had in order to follow him. He warned them that they would have to sit loose—very loose indeed—to natural ties and affections. 'If any one comes to me and does not hate his own father and mother and wife and children and brothers and sisters, yes, and even his own life, he cannot be my disciple.'[1] It was not to an isolated individual but to the whole of his 'little flock' that he said: 'Sell your possessions, and give alms; provide yourselves with purses that do not grow old, with a treasure in the heavens that does not fail.'[2] He told them to have no care for food or clothing or earthly goods and to take no thought for the morrow. In other words, he forbade them to be concerned with most of the things with which men of the world and the nations of the world are invariably and inevitably concerned. Likewise, he forbade his disciples to assert their rights or to seek high places. He told them not to take oaths, not to resist evil, to give to whoever asked. What could be more nonconformist than that?

The first followers of Christ took him at his word. They did what he told them and imitated his example as closely as they could. Consequently, they were the few compared with the many. They walked in the narrow way that leads to life. They did not marvel that the world hated them. Moreover, Christ's apostles reiterated and drove home the precepts of the Master. 'Do you not know that friendship with the world is enmity with God?' says St James.[3] 'Do not love the world or the things in the world', says St John.[4] 'If any one loves the world, love for the Father is not in him.' These statements are, to say the least, as strong and as plain and as nonconformist as St Paul's 'Do not be conformed to this world', and as Christ's own words: 'No man can serve two masters . . . You cannot serve God and mammon.'[5]

It seems evident then from the most cursory survey of the New Testament that, if Christians are to be faithful to Christ, they must be in perpetual collision with the world and with the ways of the world. And is it not equally evident from the most cursory survey of the history of the church that Christianity lost its pristine power from just about the time that it finally

[1] Luke 14.26.   [2] Luke 12.33.   [3] James 4.4.   [4] I John 2.15.
[5] Matt. 6.24.

15

came to terms with the world and abandoned its original nonconformity? I mean the time when the church yielded to the blandishments of the world in the person of the Emperor Constantine. There is a legend in the life of Sylvester who was pope at that period. It says that at the moment when Constantine bestowed large endowments on the church a voice from heaven was heard to say, '*Hodie venenum effusum est in Ecclesiam*,' 'Today is there poison poured upon the Church'.[1] Must we not agree that the Christians by this fateful surrender belied their claim to be followers of the Christ of the New Testament, and have been doing so ever since?

Is it not in fact the case that throughout the major part of their history the Christians have been trying to have the best of both worlds, and in consequence have produced a caricature, not to say a flat contradiction, of the discipleship which they have continued to profess? Whereas the earliest disciples took Christ at his word, and so were as separate from the society by which they were surrounded as a ship is from the sea or as a colony in a foreign land is from the native population, after the fatal capitulation in the fourth century church and world ceased to be opposed, and before long it was practically impossible to draw a line between them. By and large, that has been the state of affairs ever since.

The case for Christian nonconformity to the world, which already seems to be overwhelming, is further supported, or at any rate illustrated, by the recurring and persistent protests there have been in christendom against the church's capitulation to the world. Groups and sects as well as individual disciples have again and again tried to recover and revive the New Testament kind of detachment and separation from the world. Was not that the main motive of the monastic movement? No doubt monasticism, like everything else in this world, proved itself to be all too corruptible. This was pointed out by a Bampton Lecturer in the reign of King George IV in the

[1] See H. Thorndike, *Works* (L.A.C.T.), i, 644.

following pungent sentence: 'While the monks of Syria were exciting a stupid admiration by a fruitless waste of existence on the top of a pillar, those of the West, in a climate less suited for such fantastic and unprofitable exercises, were employed more gainfully in amassing wealth and acquiring power.'[1]

However much truth there may be in that, it belies the original inspiration of the movement at its best, and the general consensus of historians would now allow that it was in the monasteries that the flame of Christ's gospel was kept alight during the dark ages, when without the witness of monastic nonconformity it might have been entirely extinguished. The monks renounced the riches and splendour and the luxurious elaboration of life in the world, and retired to the deserts or to monasteries in order to testify to the Christian faith that man's true citizenship is not on earth but in heaven, and that the vision of God and the life of the spirit cannot be combined with 'the lust of the flesh, the lust of the eyes, and the pride of life'. To most men the call of the unseen, eternal kingdom of God sounds faint and ghostly; to the monks it was strong and clear and overriding. They really believed that this life is but an episode, a brief journey to something better, a preparation for another life, and acting upon the belief they became social nonconformists.

Move on to the middle ages, the period when the catholic church penetrated and subdued a whole civilization, as never before or since. In those ages of faith as they have been called, when it seemed, but only seemed, that the world had been consecrated by the church, was it not really men like St Francis of Assisi who were the genuine followers and ambassadors of him who had not where to lay his head—those Christians, that is to say, who renounced the world despite its Christian façade, who refused to conform to it, and who embraced poverty for Jesus' sake? Is not the veneration in which St Francis is universally held by Christians—even if very

[1] G. Chandler, *Bampton Lectures* for 1825, p. 279.

few of us have any intention of following his example—a sign that we know in our heart of hearts that he was right about what Christianity, properly understood, means and involves?

Or, once more, consider the so-called puritans after the Reformation. It is true that they did not detach themselves from the world in the same way as the monks and the friars, or become nonconformists to the same extent. But they represent a similar protest against ecclesiastical worldliness. They took part in business and commerce and they did not renounce family life, but they aimed at keeping themselves 'unspotted from the world' by rejecting its luxuries and refusing to participate in its pleasures. They worked out an austere and devout way of life which they not only imposed on themselves, but sought to impose on the whole of society, since only in a refusal to compromise lay safety. Puritanism in its later manifestations—its rigid and unlovely sabbatarianism, its obsesssion with teetotalism, and so on—may have few attractions for us today. All the same, if we are honest, shall we not have to admit that that kind of earnest nonconformity with the ways of the world is much nearer to the Christianity of the New Testament than our own easy-going conformity?

Again, the tractarians in the nineteenth century were marked by an austerity towards the world comparable with that of the puritans in the seventeenth century, and may not that have been the secret of their appeal? Listen to Newman saying in a sermon what he thinks about the kingdoms of this world.

Earthly kingdoms are founded, not in justice, but in injustice. They are created by the sword, by robbery, cruelty, perjury, craft, and fraud. There never was a kingdom, except Christ's, which was not conceived and born, nurtured and educated, in sin. There never was a state but was committed to acts and maxims which it is its crime to maintain, and its ruin to abandon. What monarchy is there but began in invasion or usurpation? What revolution has been effected without self-will, violence, or hypocrisy? What popular government but is blown about by every wind, as if it had no conscience and no responsibilities? What dominion of the few but is selfish and unscrupulous? Where is military strength without the passion for war? Where is trade without the love of filthy lucre, which is the root of all evil?[1]

Few Christians may think or speak in those terms today, but that may be because we do not want to face the truth they contain. I have known soldiers who confessed that, if they took Christianity as seriously as it should be taken, they would have to be pacifists. Dr Inge once observed that 'like certain ministers of state, the Church has always done well in opposition, and badly in office',[2] and is that surprising if the condition of the world is even approximately as Newman described it?

The conclusion appears to be not only that the nonconformists are right, but also that those of us who would not have the effrontery to claim that we are ourselves living in nonconformity to the world, nevertheless tacitly acknowledge that such nonconformity is the authentic Christianity.

III

That is one side of the case or one side of the picture. At first sight and so presented, it may seem overwhelming. But now we will look at the other side. In the first place, ask yourself whether it is inherently probable that Christianity, in order to be true to itself, ought consistently to have renounced the world. Leaving aside the question whether consistent nonconformity and a literal following of Christ's example would not entail universal Christian celibacy and therefore the self-extinction of Christianity, I simply ask what would have

[1] J. H. Newman, *Sermons on subjects of the day* (1844 edition), p. 273 (1889 edition, p. 242).

[2] W. R. Inge, *The Church and the Age*, p. viii.

19

happened if Christians had consistently rejected responsibility for the conduct of the world, and if they had refused to share its interests and to take part in its business to the extent that the New Testament *prima facie* prescribes and nonconformists have advocated?

The church in that case might have reproduced itself, but it would have remained a small sect, living in isolation from the world and without direct influence upon it. It would have made no sustained attempt to improve the health and conduct of the world. Here are some rather hard but fundamentally just words of T. H. Green in which for 'monasticism' other kinds of nonconformity could equally well be read.

> What the sick man of modern society wants is regulated diet; and monasticism at best only offers strong physic. It does nothing to organize life. The real movement of the world has passed it by. It lets the muddy tide have its way, and merely picks up a few stones thrown on the shore, which will take the saintly polish—not without satisfaction that the tide should be as muddy as it is by way of contrast.[1]

If the Christians had been consistently nonconformist, they would have left politics, legislation, commerce and the arts to be carried on and cultivated by other men, however godless they might be. To all that we include in the term 'civilization',[2] all that trains and furnishes men for civil life, the

[1] See S. Paget (ed.), *Henry Scott Holland*, p. 31.

[2] With Dean Church I include under the word *civilization* 'all that man does, all that he discovers, all that he becomes, to fit himself most suitably for the life in which he finds himself here. . . . There is such a thing as making this present life as perfect as it can be made for its own sake; improving, inventing, adjusting, correcting, strictly examining into detail, sowing seeds and launching deeply-laid plans of policy, facing the present and realising the future, for the sake of what happens and must happen *in time*, under the known conditions of our experience here.' R. W. Church, *The Gifts of Civilisation*, pp. 109f. I am indebted to this book at various points in the present chapter.

Christians would have had to say *non possumus*. They would deliberately have refused, when the opportunity came to them, to be responsible for maintaining order, for organizing the work of the world, and for establishing the highest possible degree of social justice. There can be no tolerable political society without the recognition and therefore the assertion of rights, nor will good men acquire the power of government if they are unmoved by ambition. Yet on the nonconformist hypothesis Christians are absolutely forbidden to assert their rights or to seek high places. They are likewise under orders, as we remarked, to take no oaths, not to resist evil, and to give to whoever asks. On the basis of such precepts there could be no law or order in the world. Anarchy would be given free rein, and anarchy would be but the prelude to tyranny.

Are we really expected to believe that God intended all the hard political work, which must be done if tolerable conditions for human existence are to be preserved on the earth, to be done by infidels, if it was to be done at all? Would not that be equivalent to saying that God meant Christians to be parasites upon the life of the world at large, to draw their skirts around them so as not to be soiled by its cares and occupations, and to leave other people to do all the dirty work?

That conclusion is so unsatisfactory as to make us want to look again and to inquire whether its premises are sound. And when we look again, we should look at the whole Bible and not only at the New Testament, for according to Christian belief whatever authority attaches to Holy Scripture, or to the word of God written, attaches to the Old Testament as well as to the New. The New Testament itself not only presupposes but constantly refers us to the Old Testament.

According to the testimony of the whole Bible then, God is the creator of the world, and he made it good. The Bible certainly condemns the notion that matter and the things belonging to our temporal existence are inherently evil. It says that men can abuse those things and thus corrupt the world and bring disaster on themselves, and that in fact they have done so. But there is nothing in the Bible, so far as I can see, to say that, after the fall, the world's structures and potentialities had become intrinsically incapable of being used to the glory of God or had become intrinsically impervious to the action and operations of his Spirit.

Indeed, we can be more positive than that. For it is the theme of the gospel in both Testaments that God loves the world in spite of the way men have corrupted it, and that this is proved by his sending his Son into it to reaffirm the original purpose of the creation and to set in motion a great work of re-creation and restoration. According to the Bible, Christ's miracles of healing and pacification, by which he brought both men and things back to normal, were signs that the kingdom of God, i.e. the kingly rule of God in and over his world, was already making its presence and its power felt. According to the Bible, Christ came to be the author and head of a new creation and to bestow the Spirit of renewal on all things. He did not come merely to save a few select souls *out of* the world, but he came to save the world. And he sent his apostles and the apostolic church to proclaim this good news to all nations, so that all nations might bring their glory and honour into the kingdom of God.

Again, if we take a further look at the life of Christ on earth and at the teaching and conduct of his apostles, we find that there is another side to the nonconformist picture. We shall notice, for example, that in the person of John the Baptist, the gospels do bring before us a consistent nonconformist, and that Christ was contrasted with him precisely because he was not a recluse but mixed in social life. He mixed indeed to such an extent that his enemies accused him of excesses. 'John came neither eating nor drinking . . . the Son of man came eating and drinking, and they say "Behold, a glutton and a drunkard, a friend of tax collectors and sinners!"'[1]

[1] Matt. 11.18f.

Christ is represented as living an ordinary life under the ordinary conditions of this world. As Father Tyrrell said, 'Of the asceticism of the Dervish or Fakir the Gospel knows nothing.' Its demand for self-denial and self-sacrifice 'springs from a belief, and not from a disbelief, in the value of life and nature'.[1] The records of Christ's preaching and teaching show that he knows and understands and appreciates the facts of life, as nonconformists usually do not. It has been well said by Dr S. C. Carpenter that Jesus knows:

> the ways of fish and seed and flowers, the price of sparrows, the signs of tomorrow's weather. He knows . . . that a man must water his beasts or deal with a sudden accident on the farm if it be half a dozen Sabbaths. . . . He preaches about figs and brambles and children and beggars and fathers and sons from the pulpit of a hill-side or a fishing-boat, in common dress and workaday employ. . . . Our Lord in his Ministry had very little privacy, except what he made for himself from time to time. Too poor to buy seclusion, too greatly beloved to be left to it for long, too human, it would seem, to desire it overmuch, he lived, from the day of his unscreened Nativity to the day of his public and notorious Crucifixion, the crowded, gossip-ridden unleisured life which in this world is the invariable lot of all but a few favoured persons.[2]

To the same effect Dr John Oman wrote:

> In the life of Jesus nothing is more conspicuous than his meagre interest in specially sacred doings, and his profound interest in the most ordinary doings of the secular life. In his

---

[1] George Tyrrell, *Essays on Faith and Immortality*, p. 243.

[2] S. C. Carpenter, *Christianity according to S. Luke*, pp. 111f. This picture of Jesus, as Dr Carpenter points out, is principally derived from St Luke's Gospel, but it is to be remembered that St Luke's own personal sympathies were ascetic and nonconformist; cp. *ibid.*, p. 115.

parables the only figures from the special religious life of a specially religious time are the Pharisee praying with himself in the temple, and the Priest and the Levite turning aside on the road to Jericho—self-approving and little approved men, solitary to their heart's core. But what a varied secular procession of kings and slaves, bailiffs and debtors, and farmers and fisher-folk, and housewives and children, and all at their secular occupations, with more feasting than fasting, and more marriages than funerals![1]

Quite apart then from the text 'Render unto Caesar the things that are Caesar's and unto God the things that are God's' (the meaning of which is obscure[2] despite the confidence with which it is commonly quoted), we can see that Christ's own example is far from being so purely and simply nonconformist as may appear at first sight. And of his apostles and first followers it can be said that, though they anticipated that the world was shortly coming to an end, they took all the opportunities that were open to them of bringing his influence to bear upon it. 'The early church looked for the imminent parousia of Christ', says Professor Wilder. 'But this cannot set aside the fact that the believers were shaping a new pattern of human community and realizing very concrete social values in a widening movement which collided increasingly with existing institutions and vested interests, economic, social and political.'[3]

At the beginning, however, the church's opportunities of influencing the social order were extremely restricted. Christ's new community, though from the outset it believed itself to be the nucleus of the new creation and intended to embrace all mankind, had in the nature of things to start in a tiny way, in an upper room. When the universal church was born, it

[1] John Oman, *Grace and Personality*, pp. 75f.
[2] See Herbert Loewe, *Render unto Caesar* (1940).
[3] A. N. Wilder, *Otherworldliness and the New Testament* (1956), pp. 118f.

looked, and had to look, to an external observer like an insignificant sect, and a sect at enmity with the world.

Has not every new movement of the Spirit to begin like that? And in the case of the universal and everlasting movement inaugurated by the coming of Christ, can we not see that it had to stand out and be set in the clearest, sharpest, most challenging colours before it took its place and did its work within the general structures of the world and the total course of history? Simone Weil said that 'one can only possess that which one has renounced'.[1] The Christian movement had to be severely nonconformist and world-renouncing in its own first phase in order that it could make its distinct and otherworldly impact on all subsequent phases of this world.

Many Christians have been puzzled by the fact that Christ's first disciples, and apparently Christ himself, believed that the end of all things was at hand. Their expectation that the history of this world was swiftly drawing to a close was palpably mistaken on the plane of chronology, but it was a providential mistake. Indeed, it was not a mistake at all on the plane where the final truth about this world has to be revealed and discovered. For if the vision of the kingdom of God as the goal of history was to be indelibly fixed in the imagination of mankind, it had in the first place to be apprehended as imminent and at close quarters, putting everything else in the shade.[2]

Similarly, the nonconformist rigour of the Lord's demands

---

[1] See M. M. Davy, *The Mysticism of Simone Weil*, p. 24. Cp. A. Schweitzer's remark: 'The essence of Christianity is world-affirmation which has gone through an experience of world negation.' *My Life and Thought*, p. 70.

[2] Cp. R. Bultmann, *Theology of the New Testament*, I, 22: 'It is a fact that *prophetic consciousness* always expects the judgment of God, and likewise the time of salvation to be brought in by God, in the immediate future. . . . And the reason this is so is that to the prophetic consciousness the sovereignty of God, the absoluteness of his will, is so overpowering that before it the world sinks away and seems to be at its end. The consciousness that man's relation toward God decides his fate and that the hour of decision is of limited duration clothes itself in the consciousness that the hour of decision is here for the world, too.'

upon his first disciples is, at least in part, explained by this same need—the need that his message should at the outset make the sharpest possible impact upon those to whom it was addressed. Bishop Gore had something to say that bears on this point when he wrote:

> I think the explanation of these extreme claims for renunciation, as of the injunctions of non-resistance to injury or violence, lies in the deliberate determination of our Lord to commit his message to the world to those only who were prepared to go all lengths with him. . . . Nothing could secure this message being really delivered to the world except the most stringent method for sifting out from among men the absolutely uncompromising spirits, such as would shrink from no sacrifice, such as would come into the kingdom bare and naked. . . .[1]

However that may be, it is obvious that the first Christians had no opportunity of assuming responsibility for the management of the Roman Empire. Their good news had to make its way and win acceptance over a wide area before it could be brought to bear upon the business of the world and could demonstrate the full range of its implications. Professor Greenslade has said that during the first three centuries 'confronted by a pagan society, lacking social prestige, unrecognized and frequently persecuted by secular authority, the Church was bound to distinguish itself sharply from the world. Conversion meant renunciation.'[2]

Even so, it is remarkable that the Christians of the apostolic age, although they could themselves have no prospect of exercising political power, held a high doctrine of the source and authority of civil government. 'Let every person be subject to the governing authorities. For there is no authority except

[1] C. Gore, *Can we then believe?*, pp. 188f.
[2] S. L. Greenslade, *The Church and the Social Order*, p. 15.

from God, and those that exist have been instituted by God. Therefore he who resists the authorities resists what God has appointed. . . .'[1] So St Paul in the Epistle to the Romans. And again: 'Remind them to be submissive to rulers and authorities, to be obedient, to be ready for any honest work.'[2] There is no need to point out that the Old Testament has a high doctrine of civil government; what is most significant is that this high doctrine is reiterated in the New Testament and shown to apply to unbelieving rulers like the Roman Emperors (including Nero!) as well as to the judges and kings and priests of the people of Israel. And with regard to the social virtues generally, the apostolic church upheld the accepted ethical standards of the hellenistic world. 'St Paul and the early Christian teachers', Dr Wand has said, 'used to discourse on virtue in very much the same way as their Jewish and pagan contemporaries. We have their lecture notes in those moral codes which form so important a part of the Epistles.'[3]

The church, therefore, is not justly charged with inconsistency, still less with capitulation, because its members, as soon as the opportunity was open to them, undertook responsibility for civil government and for conducting the affairs of this world. It is likely enough, it is in fact quite certain, that the church was by that time insufficiently alive to the dangers by which its witness and its integrity were imperilled when it took the whole field of civilization and culture under its wing. In many respects it became—and remained—so much 'conformed to this world' as to give abundant grounds for the recurring nonconformist protests that have marked its history.

---

[1] Rom. 13.1f. Cp. I Peter 2.13f.; John 19.11.

[2] Titus 3.1. Cp. I Tim. 2.1f. It is true that a very different note is struck in the Revelation of St John which shows that if the New Testament doctrine of civil government is high, it is not absolutist. We know that St Paul himself on at least one occasion deliberately defied political authority, viz. when he escaped from Damascus in a basket (II Cor. 11.32).

[3] J. W. C. Wand, *The Church, its Nature, Structure, and Function,* p. 24.

It has been necessary that John the Baptist should be repeatedly raised from the dead.

On the main issue of political responsibility, however, can we doubt that the instinct of the great majority of Christians has been right even if it did coincide with their natural disposition and interests? They knew that this world is destined to pass away and that mankind has here no continuing city, but they knew also that this world is not worthless or to be treated with contempt. They felt instinctively that God wanted them to do the best and the most that they could for the earthly city, while they aspired after the heavenly.

Nor has this belief been just the instinctive judgment of the untutored Christian mind, embraced and persisted in despite the teachings of august and supposedly disinterested theologians and evangelists. I referred earlier to Dr Richard Niebuhr's classification of five different types of answer to the question of the relation between Christ and culture. And in order to make the point that the theological mind is here in broad and basic agreement with the lay mind, I will give the briefest possible summary of what he says.

As Dr Niebuhr uses the terms 'culture' and 'civilization', they are practically synonymous. Culture, he says, 'comprises language, habits, ideas, beliefs, customs, social organization, inherited artifacts, technical processes, and values' (p. 46).[1] Culture is what man superimposes on the natural. 'A river is nature, a canal culture; a raw piece of quartz is nature, an arrowhead culture; a moan is natural, a word cultural. Culture is the work of men's minds and hands' (p. 47). Christians acknowledge Christ to be the final revelation of the word and will of God; how then ought they to assess the whole field of culture with its manifold and ever-developing claims?

As I have said, Dr Niebuhr distinguishes five typical answers to this question, though he constantly warns himself and the

---

[1] Page references are to Richard Niebuhr, *Christ and Culture* (1952).

28

readers of his book against 'the danger of confusing hypothetical types with the rich variety and the colourful individuality of historical persons' (p. 126). With this proviso, he says that there is *first* the type that emphasizes the opposition between Christ and culture, which can be given the title: 'Christ against Culture'. Of this type, the First Epistle of St John, Tertullian, and Tolstoy, are examples. The *second* type see a fundamental agreement and possibility of accommodation between Christ and culture—'The Christ of Culture'; the Gnostics. Abelard, Locke, and Ritschl, exemplify various aspects of this type. The *third* type takes the differences between the claims of Christ and of culture more seriously than the second type, yet at the same time it stands for a synthesis between them: 'Christ above Culture'. Clement of Alexandria, St Thomas Aquinas, and Bishop Butler, are representatives of it. The *fourth* type, described as dualist, holds the claims of Christ and culture in a dialectical tension: 'Christ and Culture in Paradox'. St Paul, Marcion, Luther, and Ernst Troeltsch, exemplify it in one way or another. The *fifth* of Niebuhr's types, which he describes as conversionist, while it recognizes the opposition between Christ and all human institutions, nevertheless sees him as the transformer of society in history and not only beyond history: 'Christ the Transformer of Culture'. The Fourth Gospel, St Augustine, Calvin, Wesley, and F. D. Maurice, are representatives of it.

So bald a summary gives no idea of the many kinds of illumination which this classification of historical types brings out, but it is sufficient to enforce my present point which is that the great majority of Christian theologians down the ages and of Christian teachers of acknowledged genius has maintained that Christians are bound by their faith to shoulder political and cultural responsibility. Only the first of Niebuhr's five types has stood for nonconformity in the sense in which I have been using the term. It is an impressive fact that the case for nonconformity has been rejected not only by would-be

Christian statesmen and men of the world, but also by the consensus of the doctors of the universal church. Clement of Alexandria, St Augustine, St Thomas Aquinas, Martin Luther, John Calvin, John Wesley, Frederick Denison Maurice, however much they may differ in other respects, stand on one side here. Tertullian and Tolstoy do not make much of a showing on the other side, even if they can appeal for some support to the first Epistle of St John.[1]

However, I am not going to claim that the problem of what is the right Christian attitude to this world and to civilization can be solved by counting heads, eminent or otherwise. All I have done in this chapter is to open the problem up. I do not believe that it is a problem that has a single or an abstract solution. The problem we are considering is one that can be solved only in real life, where it confronts every Christian in a thousand different forms. In the following chapters, I intend to approach or to attack the subject from various starting-points or, in other words, to make several distinct journeys of the mind. I shall not be disappointed if at the end of them all the reader finds himself, as I do myself, more in the dark about some things as well as more in the light about others!

---

[1] On the teaching of I John about the church and the world, see C. H. Dodd, *The Johannine Epistles*, pp. 39-46.

II

On Living in Two Worlds at Once

I

WHEN we speak of 'the world' we may mean one of at least four different things: (i) an area of space, or (ii) a period of time, or (iii) the earth's inhabitants, or (iv) a moral quality, of which the epithet is 'worldly' or 'unworldly'. Sir Thomas Browne had in mind an area of space when he said:

> The world, which took but six days to make, is like to take six thousand to make out.

But he was thinking of a period of time when he said:

> The created world is but a small parenthesis in eternity.

Alexander Pope meant the inhabitants of the earth in the familiar couplet:

> In Faith and Hope the world will disagree,
> But all Mankind's concern is Charity.

And Francis Bacon was thinking of a moral quality when he said:

> The more a man drinketh of the world, the more it intoxicateth.

In the English Bible as well as in our every-day speech 'the world' may have any of these meanings. Its original, etymological meaning is an age or a period of time; and of the various Hebrew and Greek words that are translated 'world' in our Bibles the most interesting and the most characteristic is ἀιών or *aeōn* which likewise means an age or a period of time. The American Revised Standard Version often, though not always, translates *aeōn* as 'age' instead of 'world', for example in Ephesians 1.21: 'above every name that is named, not only in this age but also in that which is to come.'

We are used to thinking of history as divided into many distinct ages—the Ice Age, the Stone Age, the Dark Ages, the Middle Ages, and so on. According to the Bible there are two principal ages which God has ordained and which closely concern us all (as happily the Ice Age can hardly be said to do!)—*this age* (or the present age) and *the age to come*.

This age began when God created mankind and started human history. In this age men were given the opportunity of living in peace and harmony with God, with one another, and with the natural (i.e. the sub-human) creation. That is the point of the parable of the Garden of Eden. But men did not rise to the opportunity that was given to them, and paradise was lost. Men chose to rebel against God, to go their own ways, and to please themselves. Consequently, this age became a storm-centre of conflicting wills. It became, and it continues to be, an age of disorder and disease and devilry, of struggle and war and punishment, of frustration and death. The Old Testament gives us a faithful picture of this age; that is why some refined persons do not like a lot of it. In what happened to the children of Israel and their neighbours, and in what they did to each other, we have a permanent paradigm of the state that mankind gets into in this age. It is a state of wasted opportunities, of merited disasters, of precarious survival.

Nevertheless, the Old Testament does not depict this age as entirely black. Everything is not submerged in the flood. God maintains for all mankind the basic conditions that make a properly human existence possible. That is the point of the story of his covenant with Noah after the flood. And to one nation, which is mysteriously chosen out of all others for the purpose, God communicates a clearer and fuller knowledge of himself and of his law for mankind and, as the counterpart of this privilege, he makes upon his chosen people the more exacting demands.

It is in the history and the literature of this chosen people, amid the uproar and the din of this age and above the cries of its mourners and its captives, that there can be heard promises and prophecies that God is going to bring this age to an end and, instead of it, is going to bring in a new age or a new creation in which all things will be made new and his original purpose will be realized.

These promises of an age to come, to be inaugurated by 'the Day of the Lord' or 'the Year of the Lord's favour', when the powers of evil will be liquidated, can be heard or overheard throughout the Old Testament, but they are especially audible in the books of the prophets, for instance in Isaiah 65:

Behold, I create new heavens and a new earth; and the former things shall not be remembered or come into mind.

But be glad and rejoice for ever in that which I create; for behold, I create Jerusalem a rejoicing, and her people a joy.

I will rejoice in Jerusalem, and be glad in my people; no more shall be heard in it the sound of weeping and the cry of distress . . .

In the age to come not only mankind will be re-created but the natural order also; thus this prophecy ends by recalling the well-known words of an earlier promise:

The wolf shall dwell with the lamb and the leopard shall lie down with the kid . . .

c

They shall not hurt or destroy in all my holy mountain,
says the Lord.[1]

Instead of the corrupt and ruthless or pusillanimous rulers of
this age, God promises in the age to come to give mankind a
king who will reign in righteousness and who will be seen in
his beauty: 'his name shall be called Wonderful Counsellor,
Mighty God, Everlasting Father, Prince of Peace. Of the
increase of his government and of peace there shall be no end.'[2]

Instead of the time-serving priests of this age who feed themselves instead of caring for their flocks, the Lord will in the
age to come himself be the good shepherd of his people. Thus
according to Ezekiel: 'As a shepherd seeks out his flock when
some of his sheep have been scattered abroad, so will I seek
out my sheep; and I will rescue them from all places where
they have been scattered on a day of clouds and thick darkness. . . . I myself will be the shepherd of my sheep . . . says
the Lord God.'[3]

Instead of the cities of this age which become cities of destruction, God will give in the age to come a new city, a new
Jerusalem, which will be the joy of the whole earth. Thus
Zechariah: 'On that day—the day of the Lord, when the Lord
God will come, and all the holy ones with him—living waters
shall flow out from Jerusalem, half of them to the eastern sea
and half of them to the western sea . . . And the Lord will
become king over all the earth.'[4]

Likewise, in the Old Testament there are promises that in
the age to come God will give his people a new name,[5] and
will put a new song in their mouth,[6] and will make a new
covenant with them,[7] and will give them a new heart and put
a new spirit within them.[8] Indeed, he will make all things
new.[9]

[1] Isa. 11.6, 9; cp. 65.25.   [2] Isa. 9.6f.   [3] Ezek. 34.12, 15f.
[4] Zech. 14.   [5] Isa. 62.2.   [6] Ps. 96.1; 144.9; Isa. 42.10.
[7] Jer. 31.31.   [8] Ezek. 36.26.   [9] Isa. 43.18f.

All these promises or prophecies, and others as well, are certainly there in the Old Testament, but no one could say for certain how or when they would be fulfilled. The Old Testament does, however, appear to say emphatically that this age will have to be destroyed and terminated before the new age arrives, and that the Day of the Lord will be darkness for mankind, and not least for his chosen people, before it is light. In this respect Isaiah 24 is representative of the message of the prophets:

> Behold, the Lord maketh the earth empty, and maketh it waste, and turneth it upside down, and scattereth abroad the inhabitants thereof . . .
> The earth shall be utterly emptied, and utterly spoiled . . .
> Then the moon shall be confounded, and the sun ashamed; for the Lord of hosts shall reign in mount Zion.

And there was the grim warning of Amos:

> Woe to you who desire the day of the Lord! . . . It is darkness and not light.[1]

That is about as far as the the Old Testament can take us.

II

What now does the New Testament say about the relation between this age and the age to come? It says something that was quite unexpected, and that is still very difficult to take in, even nearly two thousand years later. The New Testament says that, although this present age or this present world has not been brought to an end and although the earth has not yet been utterly wasted and utterly spoiled, yet the age to come has already begun. That is to say, it has arrived during the history of this present world instead of after its close, though

[1] Amos 5.18.

it should be added that most, if not all, of the New Testament writers did believe that the end of this age was only quite a short time ahead.[1]

But whether the winding up of this age was a short time or a long time ahead, they certainly believed that Jesus Christ had inaugurated the age to come. It had actually dawned with his advent into the world. He embodied the age to come—in himself and in what he did and in what he set in motion. In him all the prophecies about the age to come were fulfilled or began to be fulfilled.[2] It is he, not the earth, that has been utterly emptied and utterly spoiled. By taking upon himself the doom that awaited the human race and by fulfilling the mysterious prophecy of Isaiah about the servant upon whom the Lord would lay the iniquity of us all, the Messiah had thrown open the gates of the new creation. The words that were addressed to the Creator in the Old Testament are now filled with fresh and fuller meaning:

Thou sendest forth thy spirit, they are created: and thou renewest the face of the earth.[3]

Through the renewing activity of the Spirit that Jesus Christ sent forth all the ancient promises about the age to come are henceforth being fulfilled. He is the king who will reign in righteousness and be seen in his beauty. He is the desire of all nations, the prince of peace, and the good shepherd. He summons all nations to come to the city of God and to prepare to enter the new Jerusalem. He has put a new song in the mouth of mankind, given them a new heart, and made a new covenant with them. The power of the 'strong man' (Satan) is

[1] On this expectation of the imminence of the end, *supra* pp. 25f.

[2] There is a rabbinic saying: 'All the prophets prophesied on one subject, namely the Days of the Messiah.' Quoted by A. N. Wilder, *Eschatology and Ethics in the Teaching of Jesus*, p. 149.

[3] Ps. 104.30.

36

breaking now before the One who is 'stronger' than he. The blind see, the lame walk, the lepers are cleansed; it is a time for new clothes and for wedding garments. The time has come and the things can be seen which many prophets and righteous men desired to see. From the day of pentecost onwards you can follow this good news being taken into all the world— the good news that the age to come has arrived and that men may enter into it now and begin at once to experience its powers and to enjoy its blessings, *despite the fact* that the present age with its painful necessities, its hunger and thirst, and its prospect of inevitable death, still goes on.

If we want to get beneath the surface of the New Testament, we have thus to try to imagine what it feels like to be living in two worlds, or in two ages, at once. Here they were still living in the latter end of the present age, and lo and behold they had also been received into the coming age. This may be what St Paul meant when he said to his Christian converts at Corinth that 'the ends of the ages had come upon' them,[1] i.e. the ends of both ages. Instead of the age to come waiting for the close of the present age, it had supervened upon it. What no one had dreamed of had happened. The old creation and the new creation were, so to speak, overlapping. To be a Christian was to find yourself called and enabled to live in both worlds simultaneously. That is what makes the faith of the New Testament so exciting, so paradoxical, and so difficult to explain. It is no good complaining of this, and asking for it to be made as simple as the ABC, for if the New Testament is right the ABC has got all mixed up with the *Alpha* and the *Omega*. The faith of the New Testament will always seem queer and unintelligible to people who are determined to live in only one world at a time, or who refuse to cope with more than one language at a time. Perhaps G. K. Chesterton put the idea into verse better than any professional theologian is likely to put it in prose.

[1] I Cor. 10.11.

For the end of the world was long ago
And all we dwell today
As children of some second birth
Like a strange people left on earth
After a judgment day.

III

Evidently, we must beware of one-sided simplifications concerning the Christian's relation to this world. We can now say that those who would be consistent nonconformists are people who suppose they are called to live in the age to come without having any responsibility for the preservation of this age. I allow that such a one-sided emphasis has served a useful and corrective purpose, since the predominant temptation of Christians is to make themselves too much at home in this age and to forget that they are also called to live in the age to come. I allow that nonconformity has a salutary, perhaps an essential, place in the Christian scheme of things. As John Morley said in another connexion: 'there is no more rash idea of the right composition of a society than one which leads us to denounce a type of character for no better reason than that, if it were universal, society would go to pieces.'[1] But nonconformists are usually enthusiasts, and so are prone to claim too much for the side of the truth that they can see and they are also prone to be censorious of those who, perhaps with less enthusiasm, are resolved to hold on to both sides of the truth.

And we must hold on to both sides. God manifestly wills this age and the coming age to exist together so long as history continues, that is, until what in the Christian mythology we speak of as the last day or the final advent of Christ or the consummation of all things. Till then we are called to live in two worlds at once, and have dual (or, if you prefer the term, dialectical) responsibilities.

[1] J. Morley, *Rousseau*, I, 50.

In the remainder of this chapter I am going to consider certain characteristics of these two worlds or ages and the relations between them by looking at them under the following aspects: (*a*) creation and new creation; (*b*) law and gospel; and (*c*) civilization and evangelization. After that, I am going to inquire whether there are positive theological grounds on which Christians ought to value highly the concerns and affairs of this age or of this world, despite its transitory character. This question of 'a theology of terrestrial values', as I have heard it called, is one that has been too much neglected by Christian thinkers and perhaps is only now beginning to receive the attention that it deserves.

However, I begin now with some remarks about the distinction and relation between:

(*a*) *Creation and New Creation.* Père Congar in his book *Jalons pour une théologie du laïcat*, published in 1954, which is an important pioneering work in this field, twice makes the point (pp. 92 and 601) that it is not only Genesis 1 and 2, as has commonly been supposed, but Genesis 1-11 that constitute the Bible's account of the creation and of the bringing into existence of what properly belongs to this world or this age. I am taking it for granted that these chapters are not historical in the ordinary sense but mythological, and that they are none the worse for that. In English we do not possess the German distinction between the words *Vorgeschichte* and *Urgeschichte*. It will not do to say that the opening chapters of Genesis deal with pre-history, since that would imply that they narrate events that actually took place prior to written or recorded history. We need a word that will denote not the opening chapters of the actual history of the world, but what every man ought to know before reading any chapters whatever of the history of the world. It is in that way we should understand Genesis 1-11.

These chapters tell us that not only the cosmos and the

natural order but also mankind and human civilization arise out of the creative activity of God, and further that in the form in which we (and all men known to history and pre-history) inherit them they have been disturbed and corrupted by evil and sin.[1] Thus, on the one hand, these chapters describe the cosmos as an orderly system which God saw to be good—the earth with its seasons and rhythms, life vegetable and animal, man and his spiritual or responsible being, the differentiation of the sexes, the institutions of marriage and of work, agriculture, technics, race, nationality, language; and, on the other hand, we are shown how these natural and necessary structures of our life have been infected and disrupted by individual and collective egotism and *hybris*, so that they can never now be what ideally they might have been. In a word, Genesis 1-11 sets before us this world and all that appertains to it as a gracious gift of God which we have ruined, but which God has not for that reason abandoned.

With Genesis 12 we strike something quite new: the divine strategy of the new creation begins to be revealed.

> Now the Lord said to Abram, 'Go from your country and your kindred and your father's house to the land I will show you. And I will make of you a great nation . . . and in you all the families of the earth will be blessed.'[2]

Here we have the new creation already foreshadowed—mythologically rather than historically, I suppose—and the first preparations for its realization already being made. What starts with the call of Abraham is to culminate in the advent of Christ and the age to come. The beginnings of the new creation stretch right back into the origins of the old: they are

[1] By 'sin' I mean that for which human beings are responsible, and by 'evil' that which is prior to human responsibility, which is symbolized by the serpent in Genesis 3.

[2] Gen. 12.1ff.

bound together in one book. Kierkegaard compared God's presence in the creation before the advent of Christ to the watermark in paper,[1] and we might say that the new creation is present in the original creation in that kind of way.

Thus, long before the advent of Christ, from the beginnings of human history, men were related to, and involved in, the age to come (new creation) as well as this age (creation). Abraham is the father of all who from the beginning had a premonition or awareness that they were called by the author of their being to something more than to perpetuate and develop the natural necessities and civilized arts of this world and that they were not for ever to be enmeshed in the hopeless ambiguity of all that this age can offer.

(*b*) Consider next the distinction and relation between *law and gospel*. The Christian who understands that he is called to live in two worlds at once will also understand that he will as long as this life lasts need both the law and the gospel. If we had to live only in this age, we should be only under the law; if we could live only in the age to come, we should be only under the gospel. But since we have to live in both ages, we have and we need both the firm, forbidding hand of the law and the uplifting, liberating arm of the gospel to do their complementary work in us and for us. As F. D. Maurice said, 'the law protests against the selfish, individual principle, and raises a standard against it; and . . . the Gospel comes to exterminate that same selfish principle out of the mind and heart of the man.'[2] It is quite true that no man is justified by the works of the law, that is, no man is brought into the age to come by anything he does or can do in this age. Life in the age to come is bestowed by God as sheer gift, but this is not to say that Christians are dispensed from the law or can dispense with it. Here is what John Wesley said on the subject: 'I cannot

---

[1] S. Kierkegaard, *Journals*, pp. 324f.
[2] F. D. Maurice, *The Kingdom of Christ* (Everyman Ed.), II, p. 210.

spare the law one moment, any more than I can spare Christ: seeing I now want it as much, to keep me to Christ, as ever I wanted it to bring me to him. . . . Indeed, each is continually sending me to the other, the law to Christ, and Christ to the law.'[1]

Law is a complicated concept with many ramifications. In the Bible and in theology it means fundamentally God's communication to mankind of knowledge of himself and, in particular, of his will for us, knowledge of what we ought to do and of what we ought not to do individually and corporately. There are various stages or levels in God's communication of his will.

First, there is that sense of moral obligation and of social duty which, in more or less rudimentary form, is characteristic of man as man even in his fallen state, and which Christians believe to be God-implanted. In the Bible this primordial 'law of nature',[2] as it may be called, is symbolized by God's communication of his will to Noah who represents the whole human race. Charles Kingsley brought out this point well in a sermon on 'The Noachic Covenant'.

> Herein lies the ground of all religion and of all society— in the covenant which God made with Noah; and just as it is in vain for a man to pretend to be a scholar when he does not even know his letters, so it is mockery for a man to pretend to be a converted Christian man who knows not even so much as was commanded to Noah and his sons. He who has not learnt to love, honour, and succour his own family—he who has not learnt to work in honest and manful industry—he who has not learnt to look beyond this earth,

---

[1] J. Wesley, on 'The Original, Nature, Properties and Use of the Law' in *Works* (1811 edition), VIII, p. 141.

[2] See C. H. Dodd on 'Natural Law in the Bible' in *Theology*, May and June, 1946; and *Natural Law: a Christian Reconsideration*, edited by A. R. Vidler and W. A. Whitehouse (1946).

and its chance, and its customs, and its glittering outside, and see and trust in a great, wise, loving God, by whose will every tree grows and every shower falls, what is Christianity to him? He has to learn the first principles which were delivered to Noah, and which not even the heathen and the savage have utterly forgotten.[1]

Then, secondly, there is the mosaic law, best known to us as it is summarized in the 'ten commandments'.[2] This was a fuller communication of God's will to his chosen people, the implications of which were progressively drawn out and insisted upon by the prophets and priests of Israel, so that it became a complete cultural pattern and code of ethics.

Finally, there is the law of Christ, which again is best known to us as it is summarized in the 'sermon on the mount'. The law of Christ, if its utterly exacting demands are not glossed, carries the revelation of God's will for human life to such searching lengths as to leave us in no doubt that this world or this age cannot live up to it or be carried on by its standards. Any nation that tried to order its affairs according to the sermon on the mount would quickly disappear or be swallowed up, and it would not be able to secure the survival of any nonconformists either. As has been said: 'the renunciation of power (which is a postulate of the sermon on the mount) carries us into a sphere beyond history'.[3] The law of Christ is in fact the law of the age to come. He himself not only taught it but lived it out to its logical conclusion; consequently he was annihilated in history by the powers of this age and carried his work into 'a sphere beyond history'.

That was his vocation as Messiah, and out of what he did as Messiah there sprang the gospel—the good news that God

[1] C. Kingsley, *Village Sermons* (1913 edition), p. 88.

[2] See Chapter IV, *infra*.

[3] *Christian News-Letter*, Supplement No. 212, 'Christianity and Power' (12th July, 1944).

had accepted the Messiah's sacrificial identification of himself with the fate of mankind in this age as the ground on which to throw open, while this age still continues, a real participation in the life of the age to come of which the only law is the law of perfect love. Thus the kingdom of heaven has been opened to all believers. But because we are still called to live in this world, we are still responsible for maintaining the law of God in its rudimentary, external and coercive forms, and are not yet *solely* concerned with its final form as proclaimed by Christ where the only compulsion it knows is the inner compulsion of love.

In other words, we still have to do with those noachic and mosaic laws which, in this age, are safeguards of the security and welfare of national communities and of the training of individual persons, as well as with the law of Christ in which there is revealed an ethic that carries us altogether beyond the possibilities of this age. This is not, however, to say that the law of Christ is irrevelant in this age. It might be compared to stars which always remain remote from every human realization but, like stars, it shows the direction in which mankind must look and towards which we should be moving even in the conduct of this world.[1]

(*c*) The distinction and relation between *civilization and evangelization*, to which I now turn, is closely connected with that between law and gospel. I have already explained what I mean by civilization; it includes all that is involved in preserving and developing the order of creation or this age. By evangelization I mean both the carrying to all mankind of the good news that the Messiah has come and opened the kingdom of heaven to all believers, and also the building up of the universal church which is the community of those who have been received by faith and sacrament into that kingdom which

[1] For a fuller discussion of the functions of the law of God in relation to the gospel see my *Christ's Strange Work* (1944).

is the new creation, and who (as the Epistle to the Hebrews has it) 'have become partakers of the Holy Spirit, and have tasted the goodness of the world of God and the powers of the age to come.'[1]

I am not required to argue that Christians are responsible for evangelization; that is obvious. But I am required to argue that Christians are also responsible for civilization, since that is the thesis of this book. I am arguing that Christians are responsible —in so far as they have the opportunity of being responsible— for what goes on in every area of this world as well as for the inner life of the church and the salvation of souls. The Bible, if you take it as a whole, leaves us in no doubt that God is interested in the welfare of nations and states as well as of the church; he is interested in legislation as well as in love, in hygiene as well as in holiness, in work as well as in worship, in art as well as in devotion, and it is to be presumed that where God is interested Christians should be so too. It would be astonishing if it were not so, since the possibility of preaching the gospel and building up the church depends on the maintenance of order and freedom by civil governments. 'He who expects a flourishing Church in a fading Commonwealth', said Thomas Fuller, 'let him try whether one side of his face can smile when the other is pinched.'[2]

In other words, evangelization presupposes civilization. And I should further be prepared to argue (indeed I have done so elsewhere)[3] that for this reason church and state ought, in so far as historical conditions permit, to co-operate and actively assist one another in their respective and complementary tasks. Not least, they can usefully spur and check and correct one another. Christians may readily admit that the church should spur and check and correct the state. But it would be a huge

[1] Heb. 6.4f.   [2] T. Fuller, *Church History*, Book I.
[3] See *The Orb and the Cross* (1945); also *The Theology of F. D. Maurice* (1948), pp. 190-4, and 'High Churchmen and High Statesmen' in *Theology*, July, 1945.

mistake to imagine that the church itself is a pure embodiment of the age to come and so stands in no need of correction or reformation. Not only are the members of the church as individuals firmly rooted in, and inevitably attached to, this world, but the church (and this applies to every particular church) as a social structure takes much of its colour and character in any given period from the civilization with which it is associated and in which it is more or less embedded, just as divine revelation takes place in and through, and not apart from, culture.[1] The church therefore belongs to this age as well as to the age to come, and the church as well as the world is subject to corruption and needs constant reformation.

But that is not a point I have to develop in this book. If our subject were Christian responsibility for evangelization, or if we were considering the nature of the church, much more would have to be said about it. On the other hand, it is to our present purpose to observe that it would be as much a mistake to imagine that civilization is unconnected with the age to come as to imagine that the church is unconnected with this age, and I am going in a moment to say a good deal more about that.

I will sum up what I have been saying so far, and prepare for what is to follow, with the remark that during the time in which we are living, when this age and the age to come overlap and we have to live in two worlds at once, Christ is king over the whole cosmos and the Lord of history, but the fact of his kingdom and of his reigning is not, and ought not to be, overtly acknowledged everywhere. What we call 'the church' is the area in which Christ's universal kingship is openly acknowledged and confessed and is being, so to speak, explicitly (if ambiguously and only tentatively) incorporated.

[1] Cp. L. S. Thornton, *Revelation and the Modern World*, Book I, 'Revelation and Culture.'

Dr Brunner has said that the church is 'a visible adumbration of the kingdom of God'.[1]

On the other hand, 'the world' or, as some people call it, 'the secular order', is the area over which Christ also reigns indeed but in which his rule is hidden and unconfessed even where it is not positively denied or rejected. The hiddenness of Christ's reign in this area, the area of civilization, is according of God's will and design. Christ's rule over the world is meant to be unevident, so that we are not compelled to believe in him and we retain our liberty to decide whether or no we will have him to reign over us. For that reason, this age as long as it lasts is intended to have a certain autonomy and independence vis-à-vis the age to come, and the world is not to be prematurely swallowed up or controlled by the church. It follows that the medieval attempt to establish an explicitly Christian civilization was misconceived. At any rate, Christians are not bound to aim at a 'return to christendom' in that sense, and nothing that I am now going to say about the high value that Christians ought to put upon the order of creation and civilization should be taken to mean that the world ought again to be made subject to the church as it was, at least in theory, in the middle ages.

IV

The question to which I am now seeking an answer is this. If it is true, as the gospel asserts, that Christ has already overcome the world and inaugurated the age to come, why does God maintain the world or this age in existence? Why does history go on, if the end of history has in principle arrived? Does this world go on just to provide time for the gospel to be preached to all nations, and not because it has any worth of its own or because the further development of its history has any positive value? Or has the world or the present age in this time between the first and final advents of Christ, even though

[1] E. Brunner, *Eternal Hope*, p. 64.

it is doomed to dissolution at last, a positive meaning and value which we can apprehend? I need hardly remark that, if we can give an affirmative answer to that question, we shall as Christians rate our political responsibilities much more highly than we should do otherwise. I do not claim to be able to offer anything more than hints or pointers towards an affirmative answer or towards a positive theology of terrestrial values. But here are four suggested pointers.

(i) If Christ by his resurrection won the final victory over sin, death and the powers of evil, over everything in the world that is opposed to God, if as the Easter hymn says, 'The strife is o'er, the battle done', why is the world allowed to go on as if Christ had not conquered it and as if the strife wasn't o'er? Some theologians have recently used the analogy of D-Day and V-Day to explain the relation between what Christ did in his first advent and what he will do at his final advent. D-Day stands for the decisive battle of a war when its issue is definitely settled; but there follows a period during which the war continues in deadly earnest until V-Day when at last it becomes universally manifest that the enemy's power has been completely broken. The period of history in which we are living, when this age and the coming age overlap, has (it is suggested) the character of the interval between D-Day and V-Day, and it has that character however long it may last—whether the interval be short as the first Christians expected, or immensely long as our grandparents anticipated, or of quite uncertain duration as we may suppose. We can see that in earthly wars there is usually an interval of this kind, but why should there be one in the case of Christ's victory?

One suggestion is that, while Christ alone is indeed the conqueror of all the evil in the old creation and the head of the new creation, yet he wants mankind as represented by as large as possible a section of the human race to have a real and active, and not only a passive or imputed, share in his victory and in the transformation of the old creation by the new. Père Congar puts it thus: 'The interval between his ascension and his return . . . is precisely the delay that is necessary in order that what has been done once and for all in the Christ may be done by all, or at least by many.'[1]

Or, to take another analogy, we may say that Christ alone has sown the seed that will fructify in the new creation and in the seed the whole process was in principle included, but it is God's will that the saved should participate with the Saviour in producing, as well as in harvesting, the fruits. On this view, our calling in regard to the works of civilization or our opportunities of bearing political responsibility are God's offer to us of an active share in that victory over the world which is Christ's alone.

(ii) It seems obviously to be the will of God that individual human beings should normally grow up and be able to deploy as fully as possible their physical, mental, and artistic capacities. God is glorified whenever human beings do whatever they are capable of doing as well as it can be done. Anything, however 'secular' it may be, that is well done honours God, whereas if it is shoddily or carelessly done it dishonours him. So far all Christians may agree, but then does it not stand to reason that the same is true of men's collective activities and that God wills the created world, and human society in particular, to deploy as fully as possible all the capacities that he has implanted in them? It is said that Christ's first advent took place 'when the time had fully come',[2] and the appropriateness of that time for what Christ then came to do has often been pointed out. All the same, we know now that the human race then was far from having fully deployed the capacities that are latent in it as a result of the original creation. During the last two centuries we have witnessed an astonishing further deployment

[1] Y. M.-J. Congar, *Jalons pour une théologie du laïcat*, pp. 98f.
[2] Gal. 4.4.

of those capacities. May we not say then that another reason for the world's continued existence is that this age may grow to maturity and that its potentialities may be as completely as possible unfolded? If that is so, Christians are responsible for seeing that the world's potentialities, as well as their own individual potentialities, are unfolded to the honour and not to the dishonour of God.

It will follow that God's purpose for mankind is carried forward towards fulfilment in the labours of civilization as well as in the labours of evangelization, and that God can be as well glorified in the arts and inventions of industry as in those of prayer and worship. Christian minds may be as valuably employed in studying metallurgy as in studying liturgiology, and the following words of Gerard Manley Hopkins have a larger and more up-to-date application than appears at first sight:

> It is not only prayer that gives God glory but work. Smiting an anvil, sawing a beam, whitewashing a wall, driving horses, sweeping, scouring, everything gives God glory if being in his grace you do it as your duty. To go to communion worthily gives God great glory, but to take food in thankfulness and temperance gives him glory too. To lift up the hands in prayer gives God glory, but a man with a dung-fork in his hand, a woman with a slop-pail, give him glory too. He is so great that all things give him glory if you mean that they should.[1]

(iii) The last sentence in that quotation raises a further question. 'All things give God glory *if you mean that they should.*' Is it after all a matter of indifference what things you do, provided you intend them to give God glory? Or have this world and the works of civilization an intrinsic, or at least a potential, connexion and continuity with the consummation of the kingdom of God? 'The God whom we worship in Jesus

[1] Quoted by John Pick, *G. M. Hopkins, Priest and Poet* (1942), p. 118.

Christ', it has been said, 'is also the Lord of history, and . . . the growing meanings which are built into the fabric of society and wrought into tradition, custom and institutions by the toil and sacrifice of successive generations are part of his plan for human life.'[1] But has what is wrought into the fabric of this world anything directly to do with the final fabric of the world to come?

I suggest that the biblical doctrine of the resurrection of the body means that it has. There is continuity as well as discontinuity between this age and the age to come, between the old creation and the new. There is certainly discontinuity. The individual Christian who in this age has been received into the age to come still has to undergo the death of the body. Likewise, everything that belongs to the sphere of this world is destined to pass away and come to an end. Nevertheless, the doctrine of the resurrection of the body means not only that there is continuity as well as discontinuity between personal existence here and hereafter, but also that there is a continuity between what makes up this world and what will go to make up the eternal kingdom of God, or, as Amos Wilder says: 'the city of God of the consummation takes up into itself the historical life of man and its significant gains and is, therefore, by no means unrelated to our life in this age.'[2] The least we can say is that it is *this* world and not any sort of world that is to be transformed at the final consummation into the world to come. In St Paul's Epistle to the Romans there is the promise that creation itself is to be 'set free from its bondage to decay' and to have 'the glorious freedom of the children of God'.[3] Creation here includes not only man's civilization but apparently the whole natural cosmos, and this promise is attested elsewhere in the Bible.[4]

[1] *Christian News-Letter*, No. 36 (3rd July, 1940).

[2] A. N. Wilder, *Eschatology and Ethics*, etc., p. 63. [3] Rom. 8.31.

[4] E.g. Rev. 5.13; for other references see Congar, *op. cit.*, p. 122.

Perhaps an illustration[1] will suggest the relation between the partial, provisional, transitory, incomplete and even incoherent achievements of civilization and that consummation into which they will at last be taken up. Consider the members of a great orchestra practising individually and in sections with a view to a concert or, better still, tuning up before playing a symphony. There are, in various degrees, beginnings of melody, but they are fragmentary and inchoate. Then at last as the conductor holds the orchestra at rest, the supreme instrument announces the theme which will sound throughout the symphony. So in man's collective as well as individual life we have, amid what is discordant and unpromising, some lovely snatches which enable us to anticipate what is to come and even to have a foretaste of it. Although these snatches and sectional essays are fitful and abortive, they are destined, after the break and rest of death and doomsday, to be taken up and included in the eternal symphony of the consummation.

(iv) Finally however, we must not close our eyes to the darker prospect. A theology of terrestrial values which depended on there being a happy ending to terrestrial history, a kind of splendid last rehearsal before the celestial consummation, would be precarious indeed. There is no guarantee in the Bible that in the period between the advents of our Lord the eternal symphony will be progressively audible throughout the world, nor that, as time goes on, the old creation will become more fit to be taken up into the new creation. Nor has such an expectation a sanction in experience. Mary Drew, Mr Gladstone's daughter, once compared human beings to heaps of melting snow in which more and more black spots keep coming out.[2] John Morley disapproved of the comparison, but alas! we can now realize only too well that the deployment of the capacities of this world, its inventions and

[1] I got the idea of this from E. K. Talbot, *Retreat Addresses*, p. 155.
[2] See F. W. Hirst, *In the Golden Days*, p. 182.

its industry, are as likely as not to issue in disaster and despair, and Mrs Drew's simile will strike us as unduly mild. A claim to find meaning in the continuing life of this world which did not take that darker prospect into account would be unrealistic. After all, there are plain intimations in the New Testament as well as in the Old that the last day, the day of the Lord, may be darkness and not light.

Father Tyrrell pointed out that 'he who said "The night cometh", gave it as a motive for working while it was yet day.'[1] And on another occasion Tyrrell said: 'This world is not the place where we are to look for the ideal. Here and there little glimpses of it are given us to whet our appetite for higher things, and to lead us from dissatisfaction to dissatisfaction, and thence to a desire for the great archetype of all ideals, in whom at last and alone the Real and the Ideal are identified.'[2] This may give us a clue to a theology of terrestrial values that reckons with the darkest prospect.

The last truth about our individual achievements in this age, however excellent and worthwhile they may have been, is that in the end we have to acknowledge there is nothing more that we can do. The tide of life is running out. Our earthly habitation is failing us. We are helpless, and our only hope lies in having something done to us. Thus at last we may each be brought to say with the Spirit and the bride of the Apocalypse: 'Come; even so, come, Lord Jesus'.[3] Likewise, the last truth about the whole human race may be that at the end of all its finest experiments and achievements in civilization it will be confronted with the spectacle of universal failure and disaster, and will have to confess that it is helpless and can do no more, that its only hope lies in having something done to it. So the history of this world will close like the Bible with the cry: 'Come, Lord Jesus.' And then he will come in power and great glory.

[1] G. Tyrrell, *Christianity at the Cross Roads*, p. 167.
[2] G. Tyrrell, *Hard Sayings*, p. 375. [3] Rev. 22 *ad fin.*

Come forth out of thy royal chambers, O Prince of all the kings of the earth; put on the visible robes of thy imperial majesty, take up that unlimited sceptre which thy Almighty Father hath bequeathed thee; for now the voice of thy bride calls thee, and all creatures sigh to be renewed.[1]

Take me to you, imprison me; for I,
Except you enthrall me, never shall be free,
Nor ever chaste, except you ravish me.[2]

It is an article of the Christian faith that the eternal kingdom of God and the consummation of all things will be not the fruit of human efforts but a gift from on high. Our hopes and expectations are to be fixed not upon a final ascent of humanity but upon the final advent of Christ. But the fact that the consummation will be pure gift does not mean that our human efforts and all the labour we shall have expended in and on the present age will have been valueless or in vain. Here is a parable to conclude with:

A teacher has given a pupil a number of very difficult problems to work out. The pupil will not be able to solve them, although he will be able to make approaches to a solution of them and to that end will increase his efforts. The solution will be given him by the teacher, but only when, through striving for it, he will have developed his spiritual and other capacities in a way that he would never even have dreamed of if the solution had been given him immediately.[3]

[1] Attributed to John Milton in *Daily Prayer* by E. Milner-White and G. W. Briggs, p. 177.

[2] John Donne, *Holy Sonnets*, XIV.

[3] Père Malevez quoted in Congar, *op. cit.*, pp. 139. Père Malevez added this reflection: 'Le disciple se sera, de quelque manière, mis de niveau avec la solution; il ne le *recevra* vraiment que parce que, dans son effort vers elle, il se sera comme dilaté à sa mesure.'

III

Are We also Among the Prophets?

I

'THE Apostle thought it necessary that the prophetic gift should continue in all the Church until the final coming.'[1] So wrote a second-century Christian. We do not know to which apostle he was referring, but evidently this writer himself believed that the whole church of Christ is intended to have a prophetic gift as long as history lasts. Do Christians today believe that? What do we mean by 'prophecy'? Is 'the prophetic gift' one that is conferred only on rare and abnormal individuals, or is it a gift that has now been canalized in official channels, or is it a gift in which all Christians have a share? Are we also among the prophets?

There may exist some enlightening literature on this subject, but if so I have not succeeded in discovering it. There is of course a large volume of literature about the Hebrew prophets, and I shall have something to say about Hebrew prophecy presently. But my main purpose in this chapter is to find out what I can about *Christian* prophecy, since I suspect there is something here that has an important bearing on the question: how can Christians discover what they ought to do with respect to this world, especially in the wide sphere of political responsibility where the path of duty is seldom plainly signposted?

I said that there is a large volume of literature about the

---

[1] See Eusebius, *H.E.*, V, 17, 4.

Hebrew prophets. Substantially less interest, however, seems to be taken in them now, except by a few expert scholars, than was the case when I started studying theology after the first world war. We were then told that the message of the prophets was far and away the most important thing in the Old Testament. My recollection that this is what we were told is confirmed by the fact that Bishop Gore, one of the most influential theologians of that period, says in his book *Belief in God*, published in 1921, that the claim of the Hebrew prophets to speak in the name of God was a crucial question which dominated the intellectual situation.[1] I do not hear theologians saying that now, and if their estimate of the importance of Hebrew prophecy has declined it is hardly to be expected that they will display much interest in *Christian* prophecy.

The English word 'prophet', like its counterparts in other languages, has been used with several meanings. The root idea of the word is not, as many people imagine, one who predicts future events, but one who speaks for God as an inspired interpreter of his will. As regards a modern definition, Professor A. D. Nock perhaps hit the mark when he wrote: 'by the term prophet we mean a man who experiences a sudden and profound dissatisfaction with things as they are, is fired with a new idea, and launches out on a new path in a sincere conviction that he has been led by something external and objective.'[2] There is nothing in this definition about foretelling the future. But the formula, on which I was brought up, that the Hebrew prophets were not 'foretellers' but 'forthtellers' is too slick. There is, as we shall see, a definite element of prediction in both Hebrew and Christian prophecy. Nevertheless, the reason why I am bringing a consideration of prophecy into this book is not that we have here a neglected means of foresight or prognostication, but that we may have here a neglected or insufficiently realized means of insight.

In this chapter I propose to consider: first, the nature of

[1] C. Gore, *Belief in God*, p. 97.   [2] A. D. Nock, *Conversion*, pp. 2f.

Hebrew prophecy according to the Old Testament; secondly, the nature of Christian prophecy according to the New Testament; thirdly, what happened to prophecy in the course of church history; and fourthly, what prophecy ought to mean in Christian experience today.

II

The origins of what is called prophecy in the Old Testament, like the origins of most things, are shrouded in obscurity, but it is generally agreed that its origins were very humble or, perhaps we should say, very crude. The earliest kind of prophecy, which was by no means peculiar to the Hebrews,[1] was probably ecstatic; the prophets were popularly regarded as closely akin to madmen. Principal Elmslie describes them as a feature of Canaanite religion—'men who—perhaps singly but usually collectively—worked themselves up to an ecstacy of enthusiasm in honour of the God. These psychic persons were called *prophets* ("spokesmen for God"), because their shouts and utterances when in the hypnotic state were deemed to be supernaturally imparted by the God whose energy (*ruach*) had possessed them, or because (restored to their normal senses) they were able to tell others about a vision they had seen or a divine message they had heard whilst in the trance.'[2] It appears that men of this kind were organized into guilds, and they may have been part of the regular staff of the Jerusalem temple and of the principal sanctuaries in Israel.[3] They were called upon at critical moments, e.g. when there was a question of going to war,[4] to say what ought to be done. Prophets of this kind were obviously tempted to give the answers that

[1] See J. Pedersen on 'The Rôle played by inspired persons among the Israelites and the Arabs' in *Studies in Old Testament Prophecy* (1950).

[2] W. A. L. Elmslie, *How came our Faith* (1948), p. 183.

[3] Elmslie, *ibid.*, p. 184; cp. H. H. Rowley, *The Servant of the Lord and other essays on the O.T.* (1952), pp. 104f.

[4] I Kings 22.

people wanted, and there is plenty of evidence in the Old Testament of how easily 'the sons of the prophets' were corrupted. 'Professional (false) prophets were the yes-men of government circles', says E. W. Heaton, 'who lent a halo of sanctity to the projects of the party in power . . . and made it their business to tell the ordinary citizen smooth things.'[1]

Those who are now generally known as the great Hebrew prophets (whether major or minor)—Elijah, Amos, Hosea, Isaiah, Jeremiah, and so on—represent so striking a development of the primitive kind of prophecy that it is unfortunate we have not a different name for them. I do not mean that there was nothing in common between them and the other sort. Most of the great prophets may have belonged to the regular prophetic guilds, and some, if not most of them, were undoubtedly psychic persons who experienced visions, went into trances or had other abnormal experiences. But this was not their principal characteristic. 'The true prophets are Yahweh's spokesmen, not his ravers.'[2] If Hebrew prophecy had come to nothing more than its frenzied beginnings, 'it would not have deserved our attention today', as Professor Rowley says. But, he continues, 'no movement should be judged by its Whence? but by its Whither? And if Hebrew prophecy had beginnings of little promise, it achieved heights of the rarest value to the spiritual progress of mankind.'[3]

What then was the nature of Hebrew prophecy in its developed maturity? I cannot do better than reproduce Professor Rowley's summary of his conclusions.

Whenever Hebrew prophecy was true to its genius, it was

[1] E. W. Heaton, *His Servants the Prophets*, pp. 24f.

[2] H. H. Rowley, *op. cit.*, p. 111.

[3] Rowley, *The Relevance of the Bible*, p. 57. Cp. Alfred Fawkes, *Studies in Modernism*, p. 259; 'The question of origin, so fiercely discussed by theologians, is in truth the least decisive of questions; the point is not what a formula, a function, an institution was, but what it has become. This, not the other, fixes at once its worth and its character.'

the mouthpiece of God. The prophet spoke God's message to the men of his own day and generation. Its significant content was not the distant future, but the principles God would have men live by. Sometimes the prophet penetrated deeply into the heart of God, and brought out some new truth concerning God himself. Sometimes he addressed himself to the evils of his day and generation, and summoned men in the name of God to sweep away all unrighteousness and injustice from their midst . . .

Fundamentally, the prophet was the man of clear vision, who looked on the events and social conditions of his own day with more penetrating eye than his fellows. . . . The prophet was the man of the open eye. He looked on any given situation and he saw it all. He saw through it to the end. He read the inevitable issue of things, and proclaimed it with no uncertain voice.[1]

Hence the element of prediction in great prophecy. No doubt, it was part of the semitic tradition that prophets should foretell, but there was more to it than that. As Bishop Gore said, their

announcements of what was to happen were forecasts— mainly of the immediate future—uttered by the prophets for the warning or encouragement of their contemporaries, forecasts arising out of the circumstances of the present and (this is the most important point) involved in the proclamation of the righteousness and righteous government of God. This—and not future events, except so far as they were

---

[1] Rowley, *The Relevance of the Bible*, pp. 62ff.; see also his essay on 'Old Testament Prophecy and Recent Study' in *The Servant of the Lord*, etc., pp. 91-128. Elmslie, *op. cit.*, pp. 196ff., speaks of three characteristics of the great prophets: (i) alertness to the possibilities of good and evil in human life; (ii) unflinching courage in facing the truth that deeds have consequences; and (iii) moral and intellectual integrity together with a capacity for intense emotion.

bound up with this—it was the prophet's business to declare.[1]

The predictions which are certainly an element in great prophecy are then of a quite different order from *Old Moore's Almanack* or Nostradamus. Unfortunately, as we shall have occasion to remark, for a long time Christians failed to understand this and treated the Old Testament prophecies as quasi-magical forecasts of detailed events that were to take place centuries later.

But we have not yet finished with the Old Testament. While the most striking way in which it represents the will of God as being made known to his people may be through the utterances of the great prophets about whom I have just been speaking, that was not the only way in which the will of God was revealed, nor are prophets like Amos and Isaiah the only people whom the Old Testament represents as genuinely inspired. The priests and the kings could also be inspired.[2] Inspiration, of course, does not mean that human minds and voices were used as dictaphones by the Deity, though it has been vulgarly misunderstood to have worked like that. The characteristic of genuine inspiration is that a man's perception, interpretation, and utterance or communication of the will of God are not merely the result of the exercise of his rational powers or philosophical faculties (though these are not superseded or suppressed by divine inspiration), but are due to the direct, personal influence of God upon him. As Wheeler Robinson said, a prophetic judgment involves a response to

[1] Gore, *Belief in God*, p. 90. Cp. F. D. Maurice, *Prophets and Kings*, p. 141.

[2] Cp. Pedersen, *op. cit.*, p. 128: 'Like most other communities of antiquity the Israelite community was built on the main idea that society had to be upheld by people whose souls were stronger than others', and the strength rested upon the living connexion between man and the divine powers which lie behind all earthly power. This expanded power of the soul manifested itself in different ways, creating in the Israelite community the three main types: the chief, the prophet and the priest.' For the close connexion between priests and prophets, see *ibid.*, pp. 130, 149.

God of the whole of a man's personality, emotional, intellectual and volitional.[1] A prophet says not only 'I think so and so', nor 'I have come to the conclusion that such and such is the case', but 'the word of the Lord came to me' or even 'thus saith the Lord'. In genuine inspiration insight is given men beyond what they can arrive at by way of reflection. Mr Christopher Dawson has observed that, without the element of mystical intuition in prophecy, the prophet would be reduced to the level of the wise man.[2] And as prophecy is more than a matter of intellectual perception, so it is more than a purely individual gift. As Father Tyrrell said:

The 'inferential sense' of a man of high sensibility in spiritual matters, who lives in keen and wide sympathy with his times, whose mind is as a brilliant of innumerable facets that catches rays of light from every quarter, whose pulse answers to every vibration of public sentiment, will, under inspiration, leap to conclusions, as to things distant in time and space, that will seem miraculous to those who stand on a lower plane and command a narrower outlook. It is by men of this kind, in their moments of inspiration, that the wisdom, which lies scattered piecemeal through the collective mind of a whole people, is suddenly fused together and transformed into some epoch-marking discovery analogous to those of a Newton in the physical order.[3]

One should not then draw too sharp a line between the individual prophet and the tradition and community to which he belongs and to which he is still closely related even when he stands out in apparent isolation.

[1] H. Wheeler Robinson, *Inspiration and Revelation in the O.T.* (1946), p. 195.

[2] C. Dawson, *Religion and Culture* (1948), p. 78.

[3] George Tyrrell, *The Church and the Future* (1910 edition), p. 167.

I want now to go further and to point out that inspiration is not restricted to the sudden fusings of insight in individual prophets, and that the Old Testament itself represents the will of God as being made known and communicated to his people by the law or *torah*[1] as well as by the prophets. The great prophets were in many cases raised up against the community as a whole and its official leaders, and they denounced their nation's faithlessness to God and its social injustices. Amos is perhaps the purest example of this type of prophet, an outsider, a shepherd, a layman, who was moved by God to invade the national sanctuary and denounce the established hierarchy and the current complacencies.

It is, however, worthy of remark that in the Old Testament, as it has come down to us, it is Moses who appears to be regarded not only as the first but as the greatest of the prophets.[2] As Dr Guillaume says: 'the name of Moses has been so closely linked with the Law that bears his name that the prophetic character of Moses tends to be obscured and he becomes the law-giver *par excellence*', but the Jews as a whole have always held that 'Moses was the greatest of the prophets'.[3] The precise grounds on which Moses came to be described as a prophet are matter for learned discussion, but at least his being so-called is a sign that in the Old Testament the distinction between the law and the prophets is not so sharp as we are inclined to suppose. The law or *torah* was an inspired communication and interpretation of the will of God, and prophecy had much to do with its development. The Lord is represented as speaking as definitely to Moses as to any of the later prophets, and under conditions equally mysterious. The

[1] On the etymology of *torah*, see N. W. Porteous in *Studies in O.T. Prophecy*, pp. 147ff.; L. S. Thornton, *Revelation and the Modern World* (1950), pp. 202-9.

[2] Deut. 18.15; 34.10; Hos. 12.13. See Rowley, *The Servant of the Lord*, etc., p. 113.

[3] A. Guillaume, *Prophecy and Divination* (1938), p. 98.

later prophets, for their part, called their own utterances *torah* and in the Book of Daniel (9.10) we read that God's laws were set before the people 'by his servants the prophets'.[1] Prophetic inspiration was not restricted to those who are now usually known as *the* prophets and withheld from everyone else.

No doubt, there actually was an historical figure named Moses, though it is uncertain how much we can be said to know about him, but anyhow in the Old Testament he has become also a mythological or symbolical figure. Together with those who sat in his seat—all the God-called and God-given leaders of the people—he bridges the centuries and is, as it were, a corporate personality through whom the nation received its structures of government and legislation, and its tradition of cultus and culture. 'Divine wisdom is *continuously* embodied in the holy community through its succession of recognized teachers', writes Dr Thornton.[2] It is also embodied or enshrined for us in the community's literature, in the Pentateuch[3] (or the Five Books of Moses, as they are appropriately called), in the historical writings, in the Psalms and Wisdom literature, as well as in the strictly prophetic writings. God communicated his word to his people through a unity 'of prophets with priests, of poets with lawgivers, of devotees with chroniclers, of wise men with story-tellers, and of all these again with rabbis, seers, and philosophers, and with plain men of action'.[4] In the whole prophetic movement, fathers of families and chieftains and judges and kings had a part to play,

---

[1] See Thornton, *op. cit.*, p. 203.   [2] *Ibid.*, p. 208.

[3] Referring to one of the sources of the Pentateuch, Professor Alan Richardson writes that, 'though we must guard against the romantic notion that there ever was a time when all the Lord's people were prophets,' yet 'J (whether man or group) is essentially a prophet. He differs from the great prophets of the eighth and following centuries in that he is not (in the sense in which they were) in rebellion against contemporary civilization. He is rather the mouthpiece of an inward awareness shared by many in preceding generations and doubtless in his own.' *Genesis I-XI* (1953), p. 21.

[4] Thornton, *op. cit.*, pp. 235f.

though a less striking and conspicuous part than prophets like Elijah and Amos.

I am going, for the sake of convenience,[1] to entitle the former kind of prophecy—the regular, diffused, anonymous kind—*mosaic*; and the latter, conspicuous kind—playing upon the name of Amos—*amosaic*. The mosaic kind of prophecy, just because it was to be exercised by men in official positions, could easily go bad or become stale or stagnant. Those who sat in Moses' seat could sit there too comfortably and complacently. They were liable to distort or to pervert or to petrify the truth that was entrusted to them and that God willed to communicate and unfold and make effective through them. Therefore God had to raise up against mosaic prophecy the amosaic prophets to issue his summons to national repentance and reformation, and to rebuke those who were handling the word of God deceitfully or who were governing his people irresponsibly. That is why the amosaic prophets were usually prophets of woe and of judgment.[2]

Both mosaic and amosaic prophecy were necessary in the time of the Old Testament or under the old covenant, and I shall maintain that they are both necessary still under the new covenant. I am about to ask what difference the advent of the Messiah and the arrival of the coming age has made to prophecy, i.e. to the inspired communication of God's will to mankind. But before we leave the Old Testament in order to answer that question, we ought to notice that, before it finishes, it contains emphatic promises that in the coming age, when God makes the new covenant with his people, a big change will come over prophecy.

In the coming age, instead of ordinary men and women having to depend on agents or agencies exterior to themselves for the communication and interpretation of God's will—

[1] I.e. without necessarily depending on the fact of Moses' being called a prophet in the O. T.

[2] Cp. Rowley, *The Servant of the Lord, etc.*, p. 125.

whether mosaic or amosaic agencies—everyone will partake of the prophetic inspiration. 'All your sons shall be taught of the Lord', we read in Isaiah (54.13); and in Joel (2.28f.):

> And it shall come to pass afterward, that I will pour my spirit on all flesh; your sons and your daughters shall prophesy, your old men shall dream dreams, and your young men shall see visions. Even upon your slaves, both men and women, in those days I will pour out my spirit.

To the same effect is the well-known passage in Jeremiah (31.31-34):

> Behold, the days are coming, says the Lord, when I will make a new covenant with the house of Israel and the house of Judah, not like the covenant which I made with their fathers when I took them by the hand to bring them out of the land of Egypt, my covenant which they broke, though I was their husband, says the Lord. But this is the covenant which I will make with the house of Israel after those days, says the Lord: I will put my law within them, and I will write it upon their hearts; and I will be their God, and they shall be my people. And no longer shall each man teach his neighbour and each his brother, saying, 'Know the Lord', for they shall all know me, from the least of them to the greatest, says the Lord.

How were these promises fulfilled—if they were fulfilled—in the days of the Messiah, when the coming age arrived?

III

Since comparatively little has been written about prophecy in the New Testament, what I shall say under this head is more tentative, and should be received with more caution. I have derived some illumination and encouragement along the

E

line of thought I am seeking to develop from a book entitled *The Ministry in the Church in relation to prophecy and spiritual gifts*, by H. J. Wotherspoon, a distinguished Scots divine; the book was published in 1916. The whole subject invites much further exploration.

(1) The first thing the New Testament says is that all God's promises in the Old Testament were fulfilled in the person and deeds of Christ himself. Hence the frequent repetition of such formulas as 'that the Scriptures might be fulfilled' or 'as Isaiah the prophet said'. As they stand in the New Testament many of these alleged fulfilments of Old Testament promises seem to presuppose that conception of prophecy as detailed prediction of events in the distant future which I have already mentioned, and sometimes they depend on verbal coincidences which strike us as far-fetched. It must be admitted that the early Christians attached great weight to what later came to be called 'the argument from prophecy', i.e. the argument that Christ's divine claims are proved to be true because the facts of his life on earth were miraculously predicted centuries before. Nowadays we are not likely to be so much impressed by this way of interpreting the Old Testament, but we might do well to recall some words of Frederick Denison Maurice.

> Men utter words—made, as they think, to fit an occasion —intended to express only some paltry device of their minds—which are pregnant with a signification that ages unborn will confess and wonder at . . . Our words are not our own,—we are not lords over them, whatever we may think.[1]

It may have been a perception of this fact which led the first Christians to search the Old Testament for anything, however strained, that could be regarded as fulfilled by Christ. It has been truly said that 'until as late as the seventeenth century A.D.

[1] F. D. Maurice, *Gospel of St John*, pp. 323f.

interest in the prophetic writings was almost exclusively concentrated on the predictive element'.[1] It is not however that element which here chiefly concerns us, and I hope to show that there are other elements in prophecy that are at least equally important. But before leaving 'the argument from prophecy' I would add that what the New Testament, in its constant references to the fulfilment of the Old Testament prophecies in Christ (and these references are much more constant than appears on the surface), is at bottom affirming is that the sending of Christ was no act of a capricious God, no bolt from the blue, no divine afterthought, but the culmination of a divine purpose that had been at work in all history before Christ and especially in the history of Israel. The New Testament methods of saying this may seem curious to us, but what is being said is of fundamental importance.[2]

(2) The second thing that the New Testament says about prophecy is that, while Christ is much else besides, he is the final Prophet—'the prophet who is to come into the world'[3]— in whom all that God has to communicate to mankind is revealed, hidden and summed up. Before the advent of Christ, prophecy came in fragments, in bits and pieces as you might say: various letters and syllables of the Word of God had been spelt out or perhaps only hinted at. When Christ came, the complete Word of God was uttered and embodied, in so far as it can be in this world.[4]

Because Christ was the final Prophet, the final Spokesman of God, there is, strictly speaking, no need and no place for any further prophets after him. All prophesying since the advent of Christ has been the drawing out and unfolding of

---

[1] *Enc. Brit.* (1947), xviii, 58.

[2] Cp. F. C. Burkitt, *The Gospel History and its Transmission*, pp. 200ff. Burkitt points out that there is a striking difference between the use of the O. T. that is ascribed to Christ in the gospels and that of the evangelists themselves. See also C. H. Dodd, *According to the Scriptures* (1952).

[3] John 6.14.

[4] See Heb. 1.1-3a.

what was implicit or hidden in the total prophecy of Christ, and of what will be plainly seen to be so in its full coherence at the final advent. But provided we understand that, it is as justifiable as it is convenient to speak of Christian prophecy and Christian prophets. The New Testament itself does so; it applies the terms to men living under the new covenant as well as under the old.

(3) Not only was Christ himself the final Prophet in the sense that in his life and teaching and above all in his passion and resurrection God and the will of God were finally revealed so far as they can be under historical conditions, but the advent of the final Prophet issued in a great outpouring of the Spirit of prophecy. According to St Luke, the birth of Christ was preceded and accompanied by a proleptic outpouring of the Spirit of prophecy,[1] and his ascension was followed by the supreme, pentecostal outpouring. This was what had been promised in the Old Testament as one of the characteristics of the coming age. So St Peter is represented as explaining in his first sermon on the day of pentecost.

> These men are not drunk as you suppose . . .
> But this is what was predicted by the prophet Joel,
> 'It will come about in the last days, God says,
> That I will pour out my Spirit upon all mankind;
> Your sons and daughters will become prophets,
> Your young men will have visions,
> And your old men will have dreams.
> Even on my slaves, both men and women,
> I will pour out my Spirit in those days,
> And they will become prophets'.[2]

The whole church, all Christians, and potentially the whole of mankind, henceforth are recipients of the Spirit of prophecy.

[1] Luke 1.15, 35, 41, 67; 2.26f.
[2] Acts 2.16-18. (Goodspeed's translation.)

No longer will ordinary men and women have to depend on special classes of prophets—whether mosaic or amosaic—in order to learn and interpret the will of God. Henceforth, all believers, that is, all who will believe in the Giver and the gift of prophecy, will have the power of discriminating between what belongs to Christ and what does not belong to him, since they have a share in the Holy Spirit who guides into all truth,—the Spirit who takes what is Christ's and declares it.[1] Anyone who reads the New Testament attentively will notice that again and again it is said that the outstanding characteristic of a Christian or of a member of the church is that he has received the Holy Spirit,[2] who enables him here and now to taste the powers of the age to come, which include the power of prophecy.

For this reason it is assumed in the New Testament that all Christians, and not merely exceptional individuals or a special order, are prophets or are endowed with the Spirit of prophecy.[3] So Dr Wotherspoon writes:

> One distinctive feature of the Messianic kingdom was to be that the Spirit of God, formerly given to the few, who by it were constituted prophets, should then be poured upon all; not that the gift should be more general, but that as within the kingdom it should be universal—sons, daughters, old men, young men, slaves and slave women should alike receive the Spirit and should prophesy and see

[1] John 16.13ff.

[2] As Gore pointed out in *The Mission of the Church* (p. 71): 'Christians in the New Testament are never regarded as persons who need to ask for the Spirit as if they had not already received him; but they are called upon to stir up, to use the gift which is already in them, or to abstain from grieving the Spirit whom they already possess.' And he gives the following references (p. 163): Rom. 8.9, 15, 16; Gal. 5.25; Eph. 4.30; I Thess. 5.19; Heb. 6.4; I John 3.24; cp. I Tim. 4.14; II Tim. 1.6.

[3] See Matt. 5.12; Luke 7.28; John 10.4; I Cor. 2.11-16; 14.31; 14.26; I John 2.20, 27. Cp. Gore, *Orders and Unity*, pp. 62ff.

visions and dream dreams. . . . At Pentecost the Holy Spirit came upon the whole Church: 'they were all filled with the Holy Ghost'. The prophetic gift is the direct and inseparable result of possession of the Spirit of God, and is therefore an essential feature of the new nature begotten in all who are in Christ Jesus, and is common to all Christians in measure as they are Christian.[1]

Dr Wotherspoon also points out that this prophetic gift which all New Testament Christians share is one of discernment rather than of prediction:

> Prophecy was not in the usual course predictive: it was not trance-speech; its note was not of the prodigious; its power did not lie in marvel: prophecy was a spiritual force—the force of insight into the thought of God and into the heart of man . . .
>
> It seems probable in fact that very much of what in writers of the first age is called prophecy would, if we could hear it now, present itself to us as simply the spiritual exposition of truth, keen discernment of the Divine intention, vivid discrimination between practical alternatives . . .[2]

(4) But it remains to be said that, although according to the New Testament all Christians and the whole church share in the prophetic gift or are endowed with the Spirit of prophecy, it undoubtedly contains as well a considerable number of references to a special class or order of prophets in the church who apparently possessed a gift which other Christians did not possess. For instance, in Acts 11.27 we read, 'Now in these days prophets came down from Jerusalem to Antioch.' 'Are all apostles? are all prophets?' asks St Paul,[3] obviously expecting the answer, No. We must ask therefore (a) what were the

---

[1] Wotherspoon, *op. cit.*, pp. 135f.   [2] *Ibid.*, pp. 185f.
[3] I Cor. 12.29; cp. 12.27.

characteristics of these special prophets (of whose existence and activities there is also evidence in literature subsequent to the New Testament), and (b) what was the relation between their gift of prophecy and the gift with which the whole church was endowed?

(a) It seems that from the earliest days certain Christians were endowed with the gift of prophecy—the gift of discernment and of unravelling mysteries as well as of prediction—in so marked a way that they were given the quasi-official title of 'prophet'. Probably some of the sayings attributed to Christ in the gospels were utterances of these Christian prophets, which became attached to his authentic words.[1] There was apparently something abnormal about the way in which these prophets said what they had to say, though this abnormality was not the same as the phenomenon known as 'speaking with tongues' or *glossolalia*.[2] They were presumably possessed of certain psychic characteristics which marked them off from other Christians. Everyone who is familiar with the history of religious revivals knows that they usually have the effect of releasing phenomena of this kind. These temporary phenomena are the effervescence which is a feature of most spiritual movements in their early days; as the effervescence subsides, they should be expected more or less to disappear. Wotherspoon suggested two other analogies which would illustrate how the subsidence of the more sensational pentecostal phenomena was a mark of a natural and wholesome development, not of decadence or decline.[3]

> The splendours of a dawn . . . appear because at first the sun shines through those heavier vapours of our world which lie low and thick along its horizon. They are splendid and are the fitting accompaniment of the sunrise which brings

---

[1] See e.g. A. N. Wilder, *Eschatology and Ethics in the Teaching of Jesus*, p. 39, for the view that there is an instance of this in Matt. 10.

[2] See I Cor. 14.   [3] Wotherspoon, *op. cit.*, pp. 96f.

light and life. Presently they fade and disappear, not because the light wanes, but because it has increased to the perfect day, the common light in which man goes forth to his work. Nothing has been withdrawn; only now the sun has risen above the mists and is shining in his strength.

Again, he recalled St John's figure of the Living River:

When the sluice-gates of Heaven are opened and it flows to earth, there must needs be the plunge and tumult of its first impact, and its earlier course may well be that of a cataract with foam and spray and loud rushing; for the course into which it descends is rough and narrow—at first the River must make its own path, clearing it through obstruction. As the river-bed grows deep and smooth under its sweep, the River will flow always more quietly. The full stream is perhaps less picturesque than the rapids; yet it has lost nothing of its volume and strength. And now it parts into the humbler channels prepared for its flow, and the waters spread and sink from sight into the thirsty ground. . . .

In other words, the disappearance of abnormal prophetic phenomena, as the church grew and matured, was to be expected, though what actually happened to the special class of prophets is, as a matter of history, somewhat obscure.[1]

Perhaps, early Christian prophets became too firmly established as a special class in the church with a more or less official status, a status analogous to that of the prophetic guilds or 'the sons of the prophets' in the Old Testament. If so, it was a fatal mistake. While officials in church or state can share in the gift of prophecy, prophecy itself is not properly constitutive

---

[1] A. Ehrhardt, *The Apostolic Succession in the first two centuries of the Church* (1953), pp. 84-95, suggests reasons why the Christian prophets as a formal class were suppressed, while prophecy continued as a permanent endowment of the Church. See also H. A. Guy, *New Testament Prophecy* (1947), pp. 150ff.

of an official class or order. As Wotherspoon says, 'By its nature prophecy cannot be official'.[1] Organized or official prophets, especially when they lay claim to psychic or occult powers, tend to become fanatics or frauds or mountebanks, and this is what seems to have happened to the special class of Christian prophets as it had happened to their predecessors in the Old Testament.

(b) But before this happened—before these special prophets became false prophets, or in so far as they had and continued to have a distinct and genuine gift—what was the relation between their gift of prophecy and the gift with which the whole church was endowed? Here again, I find Wotherspoon's suggestion illuminating. He writes:

> The gift is there before the use of the gift; and the gift may be possessed without its utilisation. One may compare the prophetic faculty to the musical. Every normal person is sensitive to the power of music, has some discrimination between the better and the worse in music, and some power, if the power be developed and trained, to reproduce music. But all have not musical genius, and of those who have, all are not composers, nor do all even possess the musical gift in such degree that they can be called musicians. . . . It is scarcely possible to say at what point of ability or culture any individual should be described as a musician. In a somewhat similar way it would be difficult to say at what point the possession of the prophetic gift constitutes a prophet—the prophetic Spirit is common to all Christians; it is as necessary in him who judges the utterances of prophecy as in him who utters it. But to judge prophesyings is the duty of all, and all have the capability to do so (I Cor. 14.29).[2]

If this analogy is apt, then the difference between the general

---

[1] Wotherspoon, *op. cit.*, p. 194.   [2] *Ibid.*, pp. 139f.

and special gifts of prophecy in the New Testament is one of degree and not of kind.

IV

I come now to my third main question: what happened to prophecy in the course of church history? The question can be answered briefly because after the first two or three centuries of the church's history the terms 'prophecy' and 'prophet' fell into practical disuse in so far as they signified a living gift to be exercised in the contemporary church, which is what we are here concerned with. One reason for this was that the terms were early brought into discredit through their being monopolized, or through their being allowed to be monopolized, by the special class of prophets who, as we have seen, quickly degenerated into fanatics or false prophets. Prophesying of the psychic or ecstatic kind can easily be faked, and the claim to be a prophet of that kind is one that can easily be traded on and exploited. In a similar way the word 'propaganda', which originally had a perfectly good meaning, acquired unfortunate associations and is seldom now used in a favourable sense. In so far as 'prophecy' got tied up with unhealthy or unsavoury 'prophesyings' the church showed good sense in adopting a negative attitude to the word, but the result was none the less regrettable in that its proper meaning was forgotten.

In the early centuries the gift of prophecy is occasionally mentioned by the fathers as one in which Christians as such share,[1] but these occasional allusions become more and more rare, despite the undoubted sanction they had in the New Testament. In the middle ages, St Thomas Aquinas in his methodical way discusses at considerable length the gift of prophecy which, he says, 'consists in the mind itself being enlightened so as to know an intelligible truth'.[2] In the course

[1] E.g. see Justin, *Dial. Tryph.*, lxxxii; Irenaeus, *Adv. Haer.*, II, 32, 4; III, 11, 9; V, 6, 1; Cyril of Jerusalem, *Cat. Lect.*, XVII, 37; Eusebius, *H. E.*, 5, 16.

[2] Thomas Aquinas, *Summa Theol.*, IIaIIae, Q. 176, A. 2.

74

of his discussion he remarks that 'at all times there have not been lacking persons having the spirit of prophecy'[1] and that 'the prophetic light extends even to the direction of human acts; and in this way prophecy is requisite for the government of a people'.[2] But as regards these points his discussion seems to be theoretical and not to be dealing with a gift that was actually being exercised in the church of his time.

It is to be observed that the various revivals in the course of church history that have claimed to be prophetic were of such a kind as to confirm the church's distrust of anything contemporary that called itself 'prophecy'. I mean such movements as Montanism in the second century, Joachism in the middle ages, and Quakerism in the seventeenth century (which was much less restrained than the Quakerism with which we are familiar today). There was indeed in seventeenth-century England a good deal of excitement about what was called 'prophesying', but it was prophesying of a narrow and limited kind. As Dr Nuttall has said, the 'prophesying' that was revived in seventeenth-century puritanism had to do with the exposition of Scripture regarded as verbally infallible and it became a question of the liberty of laymen to preach.[3] From the seventeenth century however there come some very wise words about the way in which God intends the gift of prophecy to work in the whole church and in the normal Christian. Richard Baxter wrote:

> Doth the Spirit work on a man as on a beast or a stone? and cause you to speak as a clock that striketh it knoweth not what; or play on man's soul, as on an instrument of music that hath neither knowledge of the melody, nor any pleasure in it? No, the Spirit of God supposeth nature, and

---

[1] *Ibid.*, Q. 174, A. 6.   [2] *Ibid.*, Q. 172, A. 1.

[3] G. F. Nuttall, *The Holy Spirit in Puritan Faith and Experience*, chap. V.

worketh on man as man; by exciting your own under-standing and will to do their parts.[1]

The fact that the words 'prophecy' and 'prophet' have not been associated with anything in the living and constant experi-ence of the great churches of christendom or with normal features of the Christian life does not of course mean that there have in reality been no prophecy and prophets in the successive periods of church history. But I do suggest that the neglect not only of the words but of explicit recognition of the gift and endowments which they denote has been a grave source of loss to the church and to the understanding of Christian belief and practice. This neglect is no doubt closely connected with the church's neglect of the doctrine of the Holy Spirit[2] in comparison, e.g. with the doctrine of the person of Christ.

One important consequence, and/or cause, of the lack of belief in, and awareness of, the gift of prophecy as a normal Christian endowment has been the clericalizing of the inter-pretation and communication of truth in the church and the obscuration (to use no stronger term) of the prophetic capaci-ties and duties of the laity. The most extreme illustration of this is to be found in an encyclical of Pope Pius X, whom the Church of Rome saw fit to canonize in 1954. In an address to the clergy and people of France in 1906 he said:

> The Church is the mystical Body of Christ, a Body ruled by Pastors and Teachers, a society of men headed by rulers having full and perfect powers of governing, instruc-ing and judging. It follows that this Church is essentially an unequal society, that is to say, a society comprising two categories of persons; pastors and the flock; those who hold rank in the different degrees of the hierarchy and the multi-tude of the faithful. And these categories are so distinct in

[1] R. Baxter, *Works* (1830 Ed.), iv, 226 (quoted by Nuttall, *op. cit.*, p. 169).
[2] Cp. my *Christian Belief*, pp. 55f.

themselves that in the pastoral body alone reside the necessary right and authority to guide and direct all the members towards the goal of the society. As for the multitude, it has no other right than that of allowing itself to be led and, as a docile flock, to follow its shepherds.[1]

No other Christian church has, so far as I know, committed itself to so extreme a statement on this subject; but would it not be true to say that, even in the case of those churches which stress the rights of the laity over against those of the ordained ministry, the rights of the laity are not, as much as they should be, taken to include the right and the duty to exercise the gift of prophecy—whether in regard to the internal life of the church or in regard to Christian responsibility in the world of affairs? Anyhow, this necessarily brief historical survey of prophecy in the Bible and the church may have been sufficient to show that there is a case for looking afresh at what prophecy ought to mean to Christians today.

I will conclude this chapter with some general remarks about the prophetic character of the church. How Christians should exercise the gift of prophecy, especially in regard to the affairs of this world, will be the subject of the following chapters.

In this period between the advents when this age and the coming age are overlapping, the Spirit of prophecy or the gift of prophecy with which the whole church is endowed ought to be working in three distinguishable ways: first, through what I have called the mosaic kind of prophets; secondly through the amosaic kind of prophets; and thirdly, through the prophetic insight and witness of the whole Christian body. When I say 'the whole Christian body' I do not mean to deny that the Spirit of prophecy may be active outside the visible

[1] Quoted by J. S. Whale, *Christian Doctrine*, pp. 133f. Cp. Congar, *Jalons, etc.*, pp. 328, 356. My edition of Denzinger's *Enchiridion Symbolorum* (11th, 1911) does not include this section of the encyclical.

confines of the institutional church or in men and women who make no Christian profession. It was upon 'all flesh' that God promised to pour out his Spirit in these days, not only on all baptized flesh or only on all ecclesiastically regular flesh! Indeed, even in the days of the Old Testament, as Mr Gladstone pointed out following Bishop Horsley, genuine prophecy was not confined to Israel: 'the agency of the prophetic order, which was employed to correct and guide the Jew, was not withheld from his neighbours: Balaam, among the Moabites, was a prophet inspired by the Most High.'[1]

(i) First then, where are we to look for the mosaic kind of prophecy now? We must bear in mind that the Jewish commonwealth was a church and state in one. Moses represents all who are by their calling and office charged with responsibility for leadership, government, legislation, education, cultus, and national well-being generally, in both church and state. The fact that, according to Christian belief, statesmen, legislators, civil servants, teachers, journalists, broadcasters—all public servants and officials and what Coleridge called the clerisy—as well as ordained ministers of the church, have a gift of prophecy available to them means that in the discharge of their responsibilities they can draw upon spiritual resources of discernment, insight and courage far beyond what can be generated out of the individual or collective human ego. They can be prophets such as the Book of Ecclesiasticus speaks of: 'Prophets that worthily upheld the name of prophecy, issuing to the people the commands their times needed, uttering, through their foresight, a sacred charge to the nations.'[2] It is gospel, it is good news, for all of us as well as for the man himself that the most seemingly uninspired holder of office in state or church can draw on a divine source of prophetic inspiration.

[1] W. E. Gladstone, *The Place of Ancient Greece in the Providential Order of the World*, p. 59.
[2] Ecclus. 44.4 (R. A. Knox's translation).

Whether or no it is attributed to the Spirit of prophecy, does not this actually happen?

> There are moments [wrote F. D. Maurice], you may all have noticed them, in the mind of the dullest, most prosaic man, when unknown springs seem to be opened in him, when either some new and powerful affection, or quite as often the sense of a vocation, fills him with thoughts and causes him to utter words which are quite alien from his ordinary habits, and yet which you are quite sure he cannot have been taught by any other person—they have in them such a pledge and savour of originality. You say involuntarily, 'he seemed for the moment quite inspired, he became another man.'[1]

Not indeed that we should desire those who are responsible for civil and ecclesiastical government to be incessantly original. On the contrary, the normal characteristic of mosaic prophecy is that it sustains and develops tradition and upholds the majesty and integrity of law. Maurice also said:

> We are often apt to suppose that a prophet or inspired man, is one who is raised above laws and government, who can lay down laws for himself, whose internal power is itself the rule for others and for his own conduct. The Scripture teaches us quite a different lesson. The characteristic quality of the prophet when he is true, is obedience. He is nothing in himself. He is merely a servant.[2]

Mosaic prophecy, whether civil or ecclesiastical, is naturally and properly conservative. That is why not infrequently it needs the stimulus and corrective of amosaic prophecy. But there is a graver need for it than that. Those who bear office

---

[1] F. D. Maurice, *Prophets and Kings*, p. 23.   [2] *Ibid.*, p. 112.

in civil or ecclesiastical government are subject to the corrupting effects of power. No one has stated and overstated more
forcefully than Lord Acton the weaknesses and betrayals to
which men are prone who occupy the centre of the stage of
history. 'Most assuredly (he wrote), now as heretofore, the
Men of the Time are, in most cases, unprincipled, and act from
motives of interest, of passion, of prejudice, cherished and
unchecked, of selfish hope or unworthy fear.'[1]

Mosaic leaders in both church and state need therefore the
raising up of amosaic prophets who will bring them and their
faithlessness, their blindness and their complacency, not only
under the criticism of man but under the judgment of God.

(ii) So then we should be prepared for amosaic prophets to
appear on the scene from time to time as long as history lasts—
inspired, disconcerting individuals who are set over against the
official organs of government and leadership and very likely
in collision with popular opinion as well. Such prophets may
arise either within the ordained ministry of a church, e.g.
Savonarola, Lamennais, F. D. Maurice, or from among the
Christian laity, e.g. Blake, Dostoevsky, Josephine Butler, or
extra ecclesiam, e.g. Carlyle, Proudhon, Marx. It is in periods of
ecclesiastical complacency that prophets are most likely to
appear *extra ecclesiam*. Mr Maurice Reckitt has called attention
to the fact that in England in the nineteenth century:

save for Coleridge and Southey at the beginning, all the lay
prophets . . ., though they spoke often in the name of God,
spoke not only from outside the Church but in disregard of
the Church. Carlyle, Ruskin, Matthew Arnold, William
Morris, Samuel Butler, Bernard Shaw—all these men . . .
were telling a complacent age some part of the truth about
the progress and civilization of which it boasted.[2]

[1] See Gertrud Himmelfarb, *Lord Acton*, p. 238.

[2] M. B. Reckitt, *Maurice to Temple*, p. 37.

Amosaic prophets cannot be produced to order either by themselves or by anyone else. 'No true prophet', says Professor Tillich, 'has ever prophesied voluntarily. It has been forced upon him by a Divine Voice to which he has not been able to close his ears'.[1] Nor is it any good our saying: 'Go to, let us have a prophet now!' All we can do is to heed them when they appear, and to recognize them for what they are, bearing in mind that the Lord usually sends them not when we want them but when we do not want them.

There is one other point that especially concerns amosaic prophecy. We are accustomed to regard amosaic prophets as men who are raised up like Elijah or Amos to denounce and rebuke the evils of their time, its complacency and its *hybris*, and this has no doubt been the most striking as well as the most necessary feature of their prophesying.

> The prophet [says Père Congar] is the man who takes his stand against all who would make the means into the end and against all who seek and serve what is merely formal and external for its own sake. He never tires of proclaiming that there is truth beyond and above any that has yet been realized. He fiercely insists that the spirit matters more than the letter. This is to say that the prophet is inevitably in conflict with received ideas and conventional notions. It is strictly the case that no prophet can be accepted in his own country or recognized by his own people.[2]

Granted that the prophet's calling is more often than not to be destructive rather than constructive, yet it may be a peculiar temptation of his, just because he is raised up against society, to be too negative or too protestant. 'The characteristic danger of prophecy as a socio-religious institution', writes Mr Christopher Dawson, 'is . . . an excess of individualism, and its liability

---

[1] P. Tillich, *The Shaking of the Foundations*, p. 8.
[2] Congar, *Vraie et fausse réforme dans l'Église*, p. 201.

to become the channel for all sorts of disruptive, revolutionary and anti-social forces'.[1]

It is the task of prophecy to build up as well as to pull down. The Spirit of prophecy enables a man to discern what is good (the things that belong to Christ) as well as what is evil, and to discern what is good in unexpected places. For example, amosáic prophets may call upon Christians to acknowledge truth which has been discovered *extra ecclesiam* and which shocks received ecclesiastical dogmas or habits of thought—and to acknowledge virtue which is fruitful though without having been sown or tended by Christian hands and which maybe bears an anti-Christian label. In one way or another, amosaic prophets are always likely to be disturbing, though they need not always be negative or destructive. And we shall not complain if sometimes they raise false alarms. 'A watchman may cry "An enemy!"' said Richard Hooker, 'when indeed a friend cometh. In which case . . . I deem such a watchman more worthy to be loved for his care, than misliked for his error.'[2]

(iii) But thirdly, it is obvious that only a minority of Christians are called to be prophets after the example of Moses or of Amos. All however are meant to be among the prophets or to have a share in the Spirit's gift of prophecy and to exercise the gift. All members of the church are capable of receiving, testing, and transmitting prophetic insight, though some members will always have a greater capacity than others, as in the case of music. We are not here concerned primarily with the rights and duties of the laity in regard to church government. If we were, I should emphasize the duty of laymen to exercise their prophetic gift in the inner life of the church, and I should commend churches of the Congregationalist order, in particular, because in the church meeting[3] they provide a

---

[1] C. Dawson, *Religion and Culture*, p. 82.

[2] R. Hooker, *Works*, ed. J. Keble, iii, p. 547.

[3] See D. T. Jenkins, *The Church Meeting and Democracy* (1944).

regular and normal opportunity for laymen to prophesy.

Here we are concerned with the question: how can laymen[1] exercise the prophetic gift in regard to their conduct of this world and their political or civilian responsibilities, i.e. all those responsibilities that arise outside the church or the ecclesiastical sphere? This is the question that will occupy us from now onwards. All I would say at this stage is that in every area and structure of the common life—in his home, his business or trade and trade union, his political party, in his hobbies and recreations and artistic interests—the layman can by thinking and speaking and acting discriminate between what belongs to Christ and what is defying him, between what is glorifying God the Creator, however inarticulately, and what falls under God's condemnation. The more we can have of this kind of prophecy, the more wholesome will be the state of this world, for the Christians wherever they are will then be acting as the salt of the earth in reality as well as in name.

I said 'thinking and speaking and acting', advisedly. The prophetic gift is first one of being able to *perceive* sharply and clearly what is the will of God. But 'prophetic illumination always involves the impulse to expression'.[2] 'A prophet is a person who believes he has been entrusted with a revelation which he is morally bound to communicate to others.'[3] The Spirit of prophecy makes those whose insight he has quickened articulate, and in this clarifying sense bestows on them the gift of tongues, and so enables them to convey and to *communicate* to others what has been given them to see. But perception or insight, however eloquently expressed and intelligibly communicated, is of no avail unless it moves men to *act* in such a way as to change something in the substance of the world. Prophecy, like other things, is to be known by its fruits.

[1] Clergymen could also of course be considered in this connexion, but their case would require special discussion.

[2] Wotherspoon, *op. cit.*, p. 138.

[3] G. L. Prestige, *The Soul of a Prophet* (2948), p. 7.

The state of this world improves or deteriorates as a result of decisions and actions taken day by day by innumerable individuals, each at his own post whether it be in a factory, on a farm, in a shop, in a government office, in a school or college. But although in the final analysis it is individuals who must act one by one in the light of prophetic discernment and discrimination, yet this is not to say that exercise of the prophetic gift is a purely individual operation. On the contrary, prophetic insight is most likely to be received by individuals not when they are engaged in solitary contemplation or are isolated in an ivory tower, but as the outcome of communion and communication both with God *and* with their fellow-Christians and fellow-men, in what we may call prophetic groups.[1] Prophetic groups, as well as, and perhaps better than, prophetic individuals, should be able to see things which other people do not see, but which other people can see too, when they are pointed out. They should also be able to see things before they have happened. If so, like the Hebrew prophets they will be foretellers as well as forthtellers.

[1] As regards 'group prophecy' in the New Testament, see the texts cited by Congar, *Jalons, etc.*, p. 468.

IV

Do the Ten Commandments Stand?

IT seems then that since the day of pentecost we ought all to be among the prophets. The Spirit's gift of prophetic insight and discernment is available for all believers. But how do we set about drawing on the Spirit's gift? Do we have to become purely passive, and to banish all preconceived notions from our minds, making them blank so that they will be ready to receive the imprint of the word of God? If we were able to do that, we should be liable to take as a divine revelation or command the first idea that pushed up from our unconscious into consciousness, and we now know too much about what lies and lurks in the unconscious to place indiscriminate confidence in its deliverances. But of course it is not the way of the Spirit to suppress the normal workings of our minds. Rather, he quickens, guides, and supplements them.

It is true that prophets receive insight beyond what they can reach by their own powers of reflection, but they are to use all the powers of reflection and discrimination that they possess. Prophets do not shut their eyes and close their minds and wait for something to happen to them. The Old Testament prophet, we observed, was 'the man of the open eye', 'the man of clear vision', who looked on any given situation with more penetration than his fellows. And there was all the difference in the world between his penetrating gaze and a vacant stare, for he had already and always ringing in his ears the great divine imperatives. What characterized a prophet was his gift of perceiving how the divine imperatives bore upon the events and circumstances of his time. It may have appeared that he was able to read the will of God *out of* the situation at which he was looking, but in reality he looked at it with a mind informed and enlightened by the divine *torah* or teaching.

It should be the same with Christian prophecy. We shall be given prophetic insight into the will of God for this world of his, if the great divine imperatives are ringing in our ears too, and our 'delight is in the law of the Lord'.[1] How then can those imperatives become audible to us? I might answer: 'By regular and attentive reading of the Bible'. That answer would be correct, but it would be too comprehensive and indiscriminate. We are wanting prophetic insight into our duty with regard to the conduct of this world. We need not turn the pages of the Bible at random. We will make straight for the ten commandments which, I believe, can mediate to us the relevant divine imperatives as faithfully as they did to the prophets of the Old Testament.

II

Ship me somewhere East of Suez, where the best is like the
    worst,
Where there aren't no Ten Commandments . . .

Kipling's lines, written towards the close of the nineteenth century, implied that west of Suez there were ten commandments, and that here there was no getting away from them. And indeed at that time, nearly everyone in England knew about the ten commandments, a great many people knew them by heart, and hardly anyone would have disputed the traditional belief that 'the Decalogue of Moses declareth summarily those things which we ought to do'.[2]

[1] Ps. 1.2.   [2] R. Hooker, *Works* (ed. Keble), ii, p. 63.

When babies were baptized in the Church of England, their godparents were told to see that they learned the ten commandments along with the creed and the Lord's prayer. The ten commandments were included and explained in the Church Cathechism which was taught to children, and to candidates for confirmation in particular. And they were constantly being heard afresh, for they were read at the beginning of every communion service. Moreover, in order that the eye as well as the ear should be impressed by them, they were displayed on the east wall of most parish churches, so that they looked everyone in the face. 'Over every altar in the christian church', Disraeli could say in 1847, 'we find the tables of the Jewish law.'[1] And about the same time Dr Pusey, the Tractarian leader, said: 'I cannot but think that the Ten Commandments, with their strict warning voice, are far more valuable to us as attendants on the altar, than images or pictures or tapestry would be.'[2] Nor was it only Anglicans who took the decalogue so seriously. When eminent nonconformist divines wanted to drive home the obligations of morality they preached and published series of discourses on the ten commandments.[3]

Thus until about fifty years ago it was impossible for churchgoers to be ignorant of them, and even non-church-goers, like the Victorian agnostics who rejected Christian dogma, did not dream of rejecting the traditional morality. Nowadays, however, the rules in the *Book of Common Prayer* directing the use of the ten commandments are commonly disregarded, and little is seen or heard of them either in or out of church. The copies of the decalogue that used to be displayed on the east wall of our churches have either disappeared or been removed to the belfry or some other obscure part of the building. One reason why the ten commandments were allowed to fall out

[1] See Monypenny and Buckle, iii, p. 69.

[2] See H. P. Liddon, *Life of Pusey*, ii, p. 477.

[3] E.g. *The Ten Commandments* by R. W. Dale; *The Law of the Ten Words* by J. Oswald Dykes.

of sight and out of hearing during the first half of the twentieth century[1] was that the idea gained currency among Christians that the law of Moses had been entirely superseded by the law of Christ and that it was now archaic and retrograde to concentrate attention on the former.

The idea that the decalogue could now be dispensed with was, as we have seen,[2] the outcome of a failure to distinguish between this age and the age to come. The law of Christ or the sermon on the mount is the law of the age to come, and it carries us beyond the possibilities of this age or of this world. In the conduct of this world we shall be thankful if the standards of the mosaic law can be realized; there is no prospect of our outgrowing its imperatives. 'We are not to dream of a *Platonic*, or an *Utopian* administration' [*sic* of this world]; said a seventeenth-century divine 'we may think ourselves well off, if we sink not into the *dregs* of social corruption.'[3] So then the Christian is not to snap his fingers at Moses because one greater than Moses has come.

I said that the mosaic law in its developed form 'became a complete cultural pattern and code of ethics',[4] i.e. for the people of Israel. Because it was so well adapted to, and so closely fitted, the circumstances of a semitic people in the centuries before Christ, it cannot as a whole be equally suited to, or equally binding upon, all peoples in all periods of history. Because the mosaic law consisted to a large extent of *positive* law, i.e. laws proclaimed and upheld by a human authority in contrast to the divine, natural or moral law, it could to that

[1] Since 1950 at least two excellent books about the decalogue have been published: *The Ten Commandments: a theological exposition* by Cosslett Quin (1951) and *Smoke on the Mountain: an interpretation of the Ten Commandments in terms of to-day* by Joy Davidman (1955).

[2] *Supra* pp. 41-44.

[3] *Bishop Sanderson's Lectures on Conscience and Human Law* (ed. C. Wordsworth), p. 265.

[4] *Supra* p. 43.

extent become obsolete. As Dr G. M. Trevelyan has said: 'if law is indeed to be the permanent rule of life to a nation, it must be apt to change with the changing needs and circumstances of society'.[1] Scholars can tell us how the mosaic law itself changed within the period of the Old Testament.

For this reason, Christians have rightly drawn a distinction between what was permanently and universally imperative in the mosaic law and what was of temporary, local or contingent force. This is the distinction that is drawn in the seventh of the Thirty-Nine Articles of Religion: 'Although the Law given from God by Moses, as touching Ceremonies and Rites, do not bind Christian men, nor the Civil precepts thereof ought of necessity to be received in any commonwealth; yet notwithstanding, no Christian man whatsoever is free from the obedience of the Commandments which are called Moral.' Gilbert Burnet accurately commented on this that 'by *Moral Law* is to be understood, in opposition to *Positive*, a law which has an antecedent foundation in the nature of things, that arises from eternal reason, is suitable to the frame and powers of our souls, and is necessary for maintaining of human society.'

The decalogue stands out from the rest of the mosaic law as a summary of the *moral law*. The great divine imperatives reverberate down the centuries in the text of the ten commandments. But in order that they may be effectively heard and assimilated, they need to be expounded in relation to our own historic circumstances. The ten commandments are best looked upon as chapter-headings of the universal law of God for the conduct of men in this world; but the chapters have to be written out again and again to meet the ever-changing conditions of human life. The best way in which I can test this claim for the ten commandments is to go through them one by one and indicate what each of them has to say to us today. But before I do that, there are some further points that I want to make by way of introduction.

[1] G. M. Trevelyan, *English Social History* (1944), p. 350.

The ten commandments are not addressed only to individual men and women, nor are they precepts only for private morality.[1] They are addressed to nations and states and communities; they are precepts for public morality. The 'thou' to whom they were originally spoken was the nation of Israel conceived of as a corporate personality.[2] Their imperatives are to ring in the ears of nations and their rulers, for they are safeguards of the security and welfare of men in their corporate as well as in their private relations. They reveal what must be done and what must be avoided if the life of this world is to be wholesomely preserved and a tolerable social order upheld. That, I take it, is why our Sovereigns at their coronation promise to 'maintain the Laws of God' and why the President of the United States, when he takes the oath at his Inauguration, places his hand upon a copy of the ten commandments. Our forefathers understood this well enough. For example, F. D. Maurice wrote a book entitled *The Commandments considered as instruments of national reformation*.[3] (I possess the copy of it that he gave to one of his sons.)

The Bible tells us that the ten commandments were written on two tables of stone. That is why the first four commandments, which deal with man's duty to God, are known as the first table, and the last six, which deal with man's duty to his neighbour, as the second table. There is an old Jewish legend which says that the two tables or tablets on which the ten commandments were written came from one block of stone and that, if fitted together, they made a perfect cube. That is a pictorial way of saying that the two tables, duty to God and duty

[1] Miss M. P. Follett, therefore, made a captial mistake when she said, 'We have the ten commandments for the individual; we want the ten commandments for the state'. *The New State* (1920), p. 333. But the remark shows how individualistically they had by then come to be regarded.

[2] On the conception of 'corporate personality', cp. my book, *The Orb and the Cross*, Chap. IV.

[3] Published in 1866. Cp. *National Religion: sermons on the Ten Commandments* by Allan Menzies (1888).

to the neighbour, belong together, support one another and make one another complete. We cannot do our duty to God if we ignore or neglect our duty to our neighbour; we cannot do our duty to our neighbour if we ignore or neglect our duty to God. It is a mutilated obedience which consists in being very religious and at the same time socially irresponsible; it is also a mutilated obedience which combines zest for improving the lot of mankind with indifference to the Lord God in whom we all live and move and have our being.

Modern study of the Bible has made it clear that in its earliest form the decalogue had no more than the opening words of each commandment. Each was a simple and direct word of command. The reasons for obeying them, or the explanatory expansions which are now appended to some of them, were added later. Thus, the original form of the fifth commandment was 'Honour thy father and thy mother'; the words, 'that thy days may be long in the land which the Lord thy God giveth thee', were added later. Although these reasons may still be instructive for us, obviously they have not the same imperative authority as the actual words of command. The Church Catechism in the *First English Prayer Book* of 1549 printed the ten commandments in the shorter form, which appears then to have been traditional, and it seems unfortunate that this form was not adhered to in subsequent revisions of the *Prayer Book*.

Finally, by way of introduction, observe how the ten commandments are presented to us. 'God spake all these words, saying, "I am the Lord thy God, who brought thee out of the land of Egypt, out of the house of bondage".' The Bible does not say that Moses, as the ruler of Israel, decided that the people should be required to observe these laws. It does not say that a commission of moralists or priests or wise men, after considering what kind of behaviour would be most conducive to human happiness, recommended the observance of the ten commandments. The Bible says that they were proclaimed by God. Their authority is divine, not human.

Just as individuals, if left to themselves, are a prey to conflicting impulses, so it is with nations. Nations are made up of a multitude of individuals and groups and classes, all of whom have their own rival ambitions and desires, interests and ideals —all of whom want to lord it over one another and to make their own will a law for their neighbours as well as for themselves—all of whom, if they could speak the Latin tongue, would say *Sic volo, sic iubeo*. The Bible is realistic about this state of affairs. It does not pretend that we can derive an agreed and authoritative standard of conduct from the conflicting passions and desires of men and nations. Left to ourselves we should be in bondage to whatever tyrant was strongest at the moment. In the Bible, the land of Egypt is a symbol of all the despots by which we may be enslaved. The decalogue is presented to us as part of the good news that the Lord God, who made us and loves us, has not left us in a state of bondage or of hopeless moral confusion. He has come to our rescue and has set us free by telling us once for all what is the right way in which we are to walk both as individuals and as nations. 'It pleased the goodness of God', as an old writer put it, 'by giving the Law . . . to make a proviso for the tranquillity of mankind.'

'I am the Lord thy God, who brought thee out of the land of Egypt, out of the house of bondage.' Here is the proclamation of the divine indicative on which all human imperatives depend. Because God has spoken these words, not only to Moses and the children of Israel but through them to all mankind, we know to whom we belong and to whom we do not belong; we know what we are bound to do and what we are bound not to do. The commandments of God are our best protection against the unjust commandments of men. On the strength of these commandments we can say 'no' both to the unruly passions and despotic desires that seek to tyrannize over us from within, and to all dictators, whether they be autocratic or democratic, that seek to tyrannize over us from without.

III

THE FIRST TABLE

I. *Thou shalt have none other gods but me.* This commandment declares who is the God that is alone entitled to men's obedience and worship. The Israelites were surrounded by peoples who worshipped many different gods and no-gods, but they were commanded to worship one God only, the God who had delivered them from bondage in Egypt and who had made them a free nation. This is the only true God—the God who delivers men from bondage. And we know more about his liberating acts now than was known then. For he not only delivered Israel from bondage in Egypt, but through Jesus Christ our Lord he has delivered all mankind from the power of the world, the flesh and the devil. This is the God, the only God, who has a right to be worshipped and obeyed.

Like the Israelites we are surrounded by people who believe in many different gods and no-gods. It is not very long since we had to reckon with the god who was invoked by the Nazis. 'We National Socialists', said one of them, 'set before ourselves the aim of living as far as possible by the light of Nature, that is to say, by the law of Life. The more closely we recognize and obey the laws of Nature and of Life, the more we observe them, by so much the more do we express the will of the Almighty.'[1] The Communists, on the other hand, do not invoke the Almighty; they deny that law has any divine source or sanction whatever. 'Law is the instrument of politics and the reverse theory is untrue', said M. Vyshinsky.[2] But there are people nearer home, possibly even within ourselves, who believe only in some sort of a supreme being, a vague kind of spirit which is over all things, but about which we cannot know anything much. Or there are people who acknowledge

[1] Martin Bormann. Quoted in *The Tablet*, 28th February, 1942, p. 110.
[2] Quoted in *The Listener*, 28th October, 1948, p. 637.

an 'absolute' or a 'life-force', whatever that may be, or whose highest invocation is addressed to 'the values of western civilization'. In short, there are lots of misty gods in which people more or less believe: gods who never do anything, who never deliver men from bondage—impersonal deities who are incapable of love and are even incapable of speech. All these curious and indefinite gods are rejected, and the cult of them is forbidden, by the first commandment. The true God, the only God, whom we are commanded as a nation and as individuals to worship and obey, is the God who has made himself known to us as a Deliverer, who has spoken to us in his Word, and has wrought mighty acts on our behalf because he cares for his people. We do not know everything about him, but we do know that, and it is the essential thing.

Thus, a Christian man—or a Christian nation—is not like an irresponsible bachelor who may flirt with any god or gods that strike his fancy. We have not been freed from bondage in order that we may adopt one philosophy of life or one moral code today and another tomorrow. The first commandment proclaims that there is an indissoluble wedding between God and his people. He will certainly care for them as a husband cares for his wife, and he looks for the same undivided loyalty in return. And this exclusive claim of God to the loyalty of men is driven home by the second commandment.

II. *Thou shalt not make to thyself any graven image, nor the likeness of any thing that is in heaven above, or in the earth beneath, nor in the water under the earth: thou shalt not bow down to them, nor worship them.* The second commandment warns us against wrong ways of thinking of God or of representing him to ourselves. Maybe we are not much tempted, as the ancient Hebrews were, and as many people still are in other parts of the world, to make and to worship idols or images of wood or stone. But we are tempted to make to ourselves mental images, our own ideas of what God must be like. God must be very, very kind, we think: he must have a blind eye. That is a false image. He cannot really be a jealous God: he must be tolerant and easy-going, and indulgent to his children as our modern parents are. That is a false image. This commandment summons us to be constantly checking and correcting our ideas of God by what the Bible tells us about him. And there we shall learn that he *is* a jealous God, which means that he cares intensely how we serve him at every moment of our lives. We cannot serve God and mammon. We cannot serve one God on Sundays and another on weekdays. The true God is a God of stern justice as well as of tender mercy, and he will visit our iniquities, our national sins, upon us to the third and fourth generation. The sins of our forefathers in the days of England's dark satanic mills are still being visited upon us. God sees to it that the callousness and complacency of impenitent communities, their pride and hypocrisy, have the punishment meted out to them that they deserve. Those that will not bow to his golden sceptre are broken by his iron rod.

III. *Thou shalt not take the name of the Lord thy God in vain.* The Bible treats names, the names of human beings as well as the name of God, much more seriously than we do. That is why Abram, and Simon, and Saul, were given new names when the great change took place in their lives. New men should have new names. A name, according to the Bible, signifies a person's character and status: it expresses what he really is. So the mysterious name of God expresses what he really is. His name therefore is to be treated with the utmost reverence and awe. Men who have no sense of the mystery in divine personality are not likely to have any sense of the mystery in human personality. The Hebrews treated the name of God with so much reverence that they would not pronounce it, but would only write its four consonants, J H V H, the tetragrammaton as it is called.

This commandment plainly condemns all profane swearing and all trifling with what is holy and sacred. A nation is responsible for any of its members who 'oft name God in oaths and only then'. The Lord will not hold that people guiltless that takes his name in vain—treats his name, that is, as if it were an empty thing, and that bandies the name of God about as though it were of no account. This commandment condemns superficiality as well as profanity. A community that fails to protect and to cultivate in its members an awareness of mystery and profundity stands condemned. A civilization, a nation, a school, an individual, that is not really in earnest about the great matters of faith and duty stands condemned. People who look upon questions about God as occasionally suitable for a brains trust or an article in a Sunday newspaper, but not as a matter of life and death, are not merely stupid or ignorant or vulgar, but guilty.

The Lord will not hold such a people guiltless. The Bible does not hesitate to speak about guilt, where we might speak only of an offence against good taste or of a lack of good sense. Men who treat the majesty of God as of no account incur guilt. Until men are appalled by the guilt they incur, they will not understand what is meant by the good news of forgiveness, which means guilt taken away. But once a man knows what it is to be burdened with guilt because of the trivial, casual, and superficial way in which he has thought and spoken of God, then he moves into the area where he can have this burden taken from him by Christ's forgiveness. A people that suppresses the recognition of moral guilt suppresses also the possibility of experiencing divine forgiveness.

IV. *Remember the sabbath day, to keep it holy. Six days shalt thou labour, and do all thy work: but the seventh day is a sabbath unto the Lord thy God. Remember* the sabbath day; pay attention to it; think what it means. For, according to the Bible, days as well as names have a meaning and a message. The six days of work and the seventh day of rest are a constant reminder that the God, who has delivered his people from bondage to forced labour, wants them both to work and to rest as free men, as men who are neither slaves nor idlers, God wants men both to share in his work of creation on six days of the week and also to contemplate what he and they have created on the seventh day. He wants men to be thoroughly active, but also to be able to be still. The seventh day is 'a sabbath (a day of rest) unto the Lord thy God'. It is a day for listening rather than for talking, a day for reading rather than for writing, a day for receiving rather than for producing, a day for the family rather than for the factory.

God has so designed men and the world in which he has set them to live that there needs to be a rhythm of this kind between work and rest, between noise and quiet, between action and contemplation. God cares about the physical as well as the spiritual well-being of his people, about the culture of a community as well as about its cultus. And he cares about the well-being of all the members of every society—for maidservants as well as for masters, for strangers, and the homeless, and for animals too. 'Thou, and thy son, and thy daughter, thy manservant, and thy maidservant, thine ox and thine ass, and the stranger that is within thy gates.' A righteous nation will see to it that all its members, not least its dumb (human or subhuman) members, have a full opportunity both of working and of resting, both of creation and of recreation.

Both drudgery and idleness are incompatible with the character of God, and therefore neither befits man who is made in God's image. That I take to be the point of the statement, in the Exodus (chapter 20) version of this commandment, that 'in six days the Lord made heaven and earth, the sea, and all that in them is, and rested the seventh day.' In the being of God there is both perfect activity and perfect rest, and men can become godly and godlike by sharing in his activity and by entering into his rest.

This commandment, at least in its extended form, is evidently coloured by the special circumstances of a pastoral and agricultural people, and its details are not to be taken too literally by us. That is the mistake of sabbatarians. In this commandment there is an admixture of positive with moral law, and only what is moral is permanently and universally binding.

In Deuteronomy (chapter 5) a different reason is given for sabbath observance. 'Thou shalt remember that thou wast a servant in the land of Egypt, and the Lord thy God brought thee out thence by a mighty hand and by a stretched out arm; therefore the Lord thy God commanded thee to keep the sabbath day.' It was by delivering the children of Israel from bondage in Egypt that God had constituted them a nation of free men; they were to set apart one day in each week as a perpetual reminder of that mighty act of God to which they owed both their liberty and their laws. The constantly recurring sabbath day was a witness to all generations that there is a Great Liberator in the world, who had delivered them once upon a time and who would deliver them again. It is well for every nation regularly to call to mind to whom in the last resort its owes its existence, its calling and its mission.

But in the Christian era, now that the world to come has supervened upon the present world, we are heirs of a greater deliverance than that of the Israelites from bondage in Egypt. We owe our life and liberty, our faith and hope, to the mighty act of God in Jesus Christ, who by raising him from the dead has proved once and for all that there is a divine power in the universe who can conquer evil and death, and who will at the last day bring life and immortality to light for the whole race of men. Christ's resurrection thus led inevitably to a new edition of the fourth commandment. One day in seven is still to be set apart as a perpetual reminder of God's delivering power: but now it is the first day of the week and not the seventh, because it was on the first day that Christ was raised from the dead, the first-fruits of God's new creation and the first-born of many brethren.

Every Lord's day speaks to us of the day of Christ's resurrection, which is the guarantee that mankind has a Liberator from the powers of evil and the negation of death. Every Lord's day speaks to us of the fact that we are living in the coming age as well as in the present age and that we can already be drawing upon the powers of the age to come. Every Lord's day speaks to us of the final day, when God's purpose for his whole creation will be brought to fruition and completion, and sorrow and sighing shall for ever flee away.

IV

The Second Table

V. *Honour thy father and thy mother: that thy days may be long in the land which the Lord thy God giveth thee.* This was originally a declaration to the Israelites that they would not prosper, or even survive, in the land of Palestine, unless they honoured their fathers and mothers. It is a warning to every nation, and therefore to us, that we shall not prosper, nor even long survive, unless we honour parents, and unless our national life is rooted in a strong and wholesome family life. But there is more than that in this commandment. The sixteenth century Bishop Hooper voiced the traditional understanding of it when he commented on its as follows:

> After and next unto God we owe most reverence unto them, of whom we have received this natural life by the help of God: and they likewise hath sustained the pains of our education and bringing up. Then under the name of the parents is concluded all other persons to whom we owe our obedience and love; as the country where we were born, or where we have our living, that we be true and faithful unto it, garnish it what we may, and enrich it with all godly knowledge, arts, and other commodities; nor to hurt it, but to die for it, as justice shall require: then the prince or magistrate, that hath the defence of the country and

the people of the same committed unto his charge: tutors appointed for youth, such as teacheth any crafts or handy means to live by: the doctors and teachers in the ministry of the church . . . also all that be our elders, unto whom we owe obedience. These be the the persons, that be understanded by the father and the mother.[1]

There is more in each of these commandments than appears on the surface. As I said, each in its brevity is like a chapter heading, and a whole chapter could be written about each. This commandment asserts that a nation is not just a vast collection of individuals, each of whom stands on his own feet, is equal with everyone else, and can do what he likes. In a nation, according to God's law, there must be a proper binding together of its members in families, and in towns and villages, and in other associations. A nation is a *communitas communitatum*. And both in the nation itself and in each lesser community within it there must be order and discipline—a subordination of some men to others, not an egalitarian rabble. There must be a subordination of the governed to governors, of scholars to teachers, of children to parents, of those who are under authority to those who are charged with authority. At the same time, those who are charged with authority, persons in power at whatever level, are themselves under the law of God and are bound to obey it. This forbids them merely to pursue their own interests or to exploit their subordinates.

Persons set in authority should regard those who are subordinate to them or who are committed to their care, as good parents regard their children; it is possible to be paternal without being patronizing. Nothing will keep men in power from abusing their authority so much as the fear of God and of transgressing the divine imperatives. 'Law and arbitrary power are in eternal enmity', said Burke. There is no authority on

[1] *Early Writings of Bishop Hooper* (Parker Soc. Ed.), p. 355.

earth so high but the authority of God is above it. With the
ten commandments in our hands we have a standing-ground on
which we can defy anyone who is attempting to usurp the
place of God.

VI. *Thou shalt do no murder*. This commandment declares
the duty of respecting and preserving human life. It is directed
in the first place against violent, unauthorized killing. It forbids
men to take the law into their own hands and for any private
reason to put others to death or, of course, to kill themselves.
It is a mistake to suppose that this commandment deals
directly with the questions of capital punishment and of war
in so far as it is legally conducted. The law of Moses provided
elsewhere for both capital punishment and war, which it would
not have done if this commandment had forbidden them.

It may be that there are now decisive reasons why capital
punishment should be abolished, and modern means of war-
fare place all men of sensitive conscience in an appalling
dilemma. But the dilemma cannot be resolved by referring to
this commandment. The sixth commandment takes for
granted the difference between private, arbitrary and unauthorized killing, which is murder, and judicial executions at the
end of a legal process or putting people to death in a military
conflict between nations which itself has as its objective
defence against an intolerable menace to human life. These
too are no doubt instances of killing, but they are not the same
as murder.

There is a positive as well as a negative side to this commandment. Negatively it condemns murder, and also we may
add any nation that treats lightly the imperilling or destruction
of life, on the roads or elsewhere. Positively it means that a
nation is responsible for preserving the life and maintaining the
health of all its members. A nation that lets some of its members have insufficient food and inhabit unhealthy dwellings,
while others live in comfort and luxury, is found guilty by this
commandment. There used to be a shocking contrast between

the death-rate in the east and west ends of our big cities, and Christians were very slow to realize that they were required by the law of God to do something drastic about it. As well as passionate murders by individuals, there is such a thing as callous murdering by society. There is a story by Tolstoy about a nineteenth-century duchess who shed torrents of compassionate tears as she watched a melodrama on the stage, while her coachman froze to death on the box of her carriage outside the theatre.

VII. *Thou shalt not commit adultery*. This commandment declares that a nation must regard as a solemn public duty the right ordering of the relations between men and women. What a man or woman does about sex is not a purely private affair or merely their own business. It comes under God's constitutional government of the world. He has made laws that are for the well-being of his whole people. They may bear hardly sometimes on individuals. They may appear sometimes to conflict with other divine imperatives, and one law may have to give way before another. But, in this as in other matters, individuals must be prepared to sacrifice themselves for the welfare of the whole community. God anyhow is concerned with the welfare of families and with securing a healthy and harmonious life for the whole of each national community. He has therefore ordained marriage as the permanent relationship in which man's sexual nature is to be expressed and fulfilled. Fornication and adultery are always guilty. A nation which treats sex frivolously and not as a sacred mystery—a nation which treats sex sentimentally and not as a matter of law and order—this is a guilty nation and it will incur the just judgment of God.

VIII. *Thou shalt not steal*. This commandment condemns not only robberies and thefts and gangsters, but all forms of petty pilfering, and light-fingeredness, and carelessness about other people's property and about public property. Stealing does not cease to be stealing because we call it by some other name such as 'scrounging' or even 'borrowing'. Stealing is not only an offence against the neighbour but a rebellion against a law of God. It is the will of God that persons should have personal possessions, by means of which they learn responsibility, and acquire an individual character—and maybe some pleasant idiosyncrasies!

The question of the rightful ownership of the mean of production, distribution and exchange is another matter. Some Christians seem to imagine that there is a universally correct answer to this question and, according to their point of view, suppose that either private ownership or public ownership is always to be preferred. But it is not as simple as that. Several things have to be taken into account. What makes for most efficiency? What gives most security and responsibility to the workers? Which provides the best safeguards against the abuse of power? And the answers to these questions are likely to be different in different periods of history or at different levels of civilization. In a primitive handicraft society the private ownership of his tools gives security and responsibility to the worker. But in a large-scale technological society private ownership of the means of production has just the opposite effect. It puts the worker at the mercy of a small group of irresponsible proprietors, and the only safeguard against this will be some form of public control, though not necessarily of public ownership.

We see then that this commandment about property will have to be applied differently in different circumstances according to the way in which it is found to work out in practice. It is a field in which there will always be plenty of scope for the exercise of prophetic insight. God commanded 'thou shalt not steal' not for the sake of property as such but for the sake of persons and national communities.

IX. *Thou shalt not bear false witness against thy neighbour*— above all, of course, in a court of law. But slanderous talk or malicious gossip, which is much more common, is equally condemned. This commandment also has a positive side. It means that we ought to have a profound reverence for truth in all its forms. We are to seek the truth and to tell the truth, not only in the law courts but everywhere. We are to accept established facts, however unpleasant they may be, and however contrary to our interests, our prejudices or our cherished beliefs. The decalogue proclaims that there is a God and a Deliverer over the world who will work vengeance on everyone—and on every nation—that maketh or telleth a lie, and who in the end will unmask every form of deception and will expose humbug wherever it may lurk.

The divine imperative to truthfulness is not, any more than the rest, to be construed legalistically. There are circumstances in which it conflicts with other imperatives. Doctors and secret service agents and cabinet ministers and others have their various problems under this heading. And it would be a dreary world in which no leg-pulling were permitted!

X. *Thou shalt not covet.* The decalogue has a terrible sting in its tail. This commandment is manifestly different from all the rest. On the face of it, they deal with outward acts which can be recognized and could be punished as public crimes. But this commandment deals with inward desires which are concealed from public view, though they are not concealed from God, 'unto whom all hearts are open, all desires known, and from whom no secrets are hid'. The tenth commandment strikes at the root and spring of all the evil in the heart of man. For the region of our private thoughts and secret desires and hidden motives is the real stronghold of our rebellion against God. However fair a face we may succeed in showing to the world, however correct our outward behaviour, there is that inner citadel where the self, the ego, craves and envies and chafes, with the restlessness of the waves of the sea.

'Thou shalt not covet' pierces that inner citadel. The best of mankind, who can say perhaps that they have put up quite a good show with the other commandments, at least so far as outward observance goes, have to confess that here they find themselves condemned. This commandment points forward in fact to Christ's revelation in the sermon on the mount of how much more is demanded of men by *all* the commandments than appears at first sight. When Christ, as it were, reads the commandments to us, he shows that in every case private thoughts matter to God quite as much as public acts. If our desires and motives are judged by this searching standard, we all have to confess that we are guilty men.

This is what happened to St Paul. It was the tenth commandment that bowled him out (see Rom. 7.7). Though as a good Pharisee he had been exemplary in his outward obedience to the law of God, yet he had not obeyed it, and he found he could not obey it, in the inner man. It was this devastating discovery of his inner guilt that convinced him that there was no hope for him or for his nation or for the world, unless he was delivered from bondage to the law, and unless there was imparted to him a kind of inward righteousness which he could never achieve by himself. It was the sting in the tail of the decalogue that convicted him of sin, and brought him to the place where he put his whole truth in Jesus Christ as the universal Lord and Saviour.[1]

In the end therefore an exposition of the decalogue brings us again to the good news of Christ's advent and the dawning of the age to come. But the ten commandments have not thereby been rendered otiose. They stand. We shall need every one of them, and much else the Old Testament has to teach us, so long as this age or this world continues to exist.

[1] For development of this theme, see my book, *Christ's Strange Work.*

V

What Does 'Z' Do?

I

IHAVE entitled this chapter 'What does Z do?' because I want now to be drawing some practical conclusions about Christian responsibility for the running of this world. I ask 'What does Z do?' instead of the more usual 'What does A or X do?' both because it *is* unusual and because Z happens to be a letter to which I am partial. Whenever I have to name a dog or a cat I always choose a name with a Z in it!

We will begin by returning to our point of departure, and then I will recapitulate the course of the argument so far, in order that we may see where we have got to. Perhaps I can best recall our point of departure, that is, the principal question to which we are seeking an answer, by noting two sayings that express diametrically opposite answers to it.

Dr R. W. Dale, who was a famous Congregationalist divine in the last century and minister of the Carr's Lane chapel in Birmingham, had many critics because of the active part he played in politics. His biography contains a chapter entitled 'A Municipal Gospel'—a title that speaks for itself. In the course of it we are told that on a certain occasion one of Dr Dale's critics addressed to him the following remonstrance: 'There are no politics in heaven; there is where your heart should be; sad, sad, that it is otherwise!'[1] The view that Christians ought to be detached from the affairs of this world could hardly be

---

[1] See A. W. W. Dale, *Life of R. W. Dale*, p. 399.

expressed more plainly. Set beside it, however, this saying of a contemporary French writer: 'The tragedy of present-day Christianity lies in its inability to see that in our times the choice between Christ and anti-Christ must be made not in the ecclesiastical or theological sphere, but above all in the realm of politics'.[1] Which of those views is right? Is the realm of politics or the ordering of this world unimportant for Christians, or at least beneath their concern, or on the other hand is it all important? Happily we do not have to accept either of those extreme answers. Our purpose is rather to find out where the truth lies between them. What have we found so far?

In Chapter I, I pointed out how strong is the *prima facie* case for Christians renouncing the world and being thorough-going nonconformists, and so for their refusing to become involved in politics and in the affairs and struggles of this world. But then we saw that there is a great deal to be said on the other side—and not only on grounds of common sense. If we look at the Bible itself as a whole, we find that it does not by any means stand for that kind of world-renunciation and uncompromising nonconformity which certain elements in the New Testament seem to call for. (I might have added that, unlike some Christians, the Bible itself is very far from despising *common sense*, witness its inclusion of the Book of Proverbs in the Old Testament and the Epistle of St James in the New Testament.)

In Chapter II, looking at the Bible as a whole, I set forth an interpretation of its message in terms of the relation between this age and the age to come, or between this world and the other world, or between creation and the new creation—the operative consideration being that, according to the gospel of Christ, we are now living in a period when this age and the age to come overlap. So we have to live in two worlds at once, and are responsible to God for both worlds, for civilization as well as evangelization, for the original creation as well

[1] Roland de Pury, *Journal de Cellule*, p. 187.

as for the new creation. I dwelt particularly on the theological reasons for our being deeply concerned with the things of this world or with terrestrial values. But how do Christians discover what they ought to do about the things of this world?

In Chapter III, therefore, I made a fresh incursion into the subject by considering the place of prophecy not only in the Bible but as a permanent endowment of Christ's church and as a gift in which all Christians share and which all ought to exercise. My reason for discussing prophecy was that I believe we are led to the conclusion that there are available to all Christians, and indeed to all men, prophetic resources of illumination not only about matters of personal conduct and personal piety and affairs ecclesiastical but also about political responsibility and the works of civilization. This conclusion is of great importance if, as I suppose, it will never be possible to provide a text-book or manual which will contain the correct Christian answers to the problems of social and political conduct that meet men daily in real life. Instead of a text-book or manual, we have something better—a share in the living gift of prophecy. Nevertheless, even if the Bible is not to be regarded as a book in which we can simply look up the correct Christian answers, can it be said to supply us with guidance or directions about the will of God for our common life in this world?

In Chapter IV, I put that question to the test by inquiring whether the ten commandments do not still set great divine imperatives ringing in our ears. The brief comments that I made on the commandments were intended not to exhaust what they have to say to us, but to illustrate how the decalogue in particular, as indeed the Bible as a whole, does convey to us an understanding of God's purpose for human life in this world. That understanding is a vitally important part of what Christians need if they are to know what they ought to do in any given situation, but it seldom, if ever, by itself settles the matter. There is a good deal more that we have to take into account before we can answer the question 'What does Z do?' or, to frame it more accurately, 'How does Z find out what he ought to do?' That is the question with which in this and the next chapter I want to come to closer grips, especially with Z's political duties in view.

Z is any Christian man or woman, though for the sake of convenience I shall usually refer to Z as if he were a male of the species. Granted that we cannot provide Z with a comprehensive text-book or manual of Christian conduct—granted that we cannot tell him in advance what it will be his duty to do in all the sets of circumstance that he will meet in the course of his life—granted that he will have to make his own decisions: still there is quite a lot of useful advice that we can give him—and perhaps ourselves at the same time—about how to sort out and weigh up the questions of social and political conduct that will constantly be confronting him in fresh forms. And since, as someone has said, 'the duty of finding out exactly what one's duty is, is of all duties the one most generally neglected',[1] there may be value in practical conclusions that tell Z how to set about finding out his duty for himself, what confusions he should be looking out for, what distinctions he ought to keep in mind, what temptations will assail him, and what reproaches he need not fear.

What a Z of real flesh and blood ought to do will depend to a considerable extent on where he is placed—in what country, in what period of history, with what aptitudes and opportunities, in what contingencies. The same kind of conduct should not be expected of Queen Boadicea and Queen Elizabeth II, nor of Brutus and the Leader of H. M. Opposition, nor of the President of Panama and the President of the Free Church Federal Council. Again, for the benefit of a man who was living in a country or in a period where there were no party politics, it would be idle to discuss the problems that arise from having to engage in them. While Z will here denote

[1] B. H. Streeter in *Adventure*, p. 77.

primarily a Christian living in Great Britain in the second half
of the twentieth century A.D., I want first to call attention to
some basic distinctions which hold good everywhere and
always.

II

Whoever Z may be and in whatever situation he is placed,
always since the advent of Christ he stands in three distinguishable relations—to God, to the church, and to civil society—
each of which carries with it a different kind of responsibility.
Many of the errors into which Christians fall come from confusing these relationships and these three distinct, though
interconnected, spheres of responsibility.

First, then, Z stands in a personal and unique relationship to
God. To God, and to God alone, he owes absolute or unconditional obedience. But that does not mean that it is possible for
him to do what is absolutely or unconditionally good. The
stuff out of which his obedience to God has to be wrought is
made up of choices not between what is absolutely good and
absolutely evil but between what is relatively right and relatively wrong, just as seldom, if ever, in real life is he likely to
meet either absolute truth or absolute falsehood. On the
sensational occasion in 1889 when before the Parnell
Commission Pigott the forger broke down under Sir
Charles Russell's cross-examination, Scott Holland wrote
to a friend:

I have never known a more exciting moment than that of
Pigott's break-down. It was one of those incredible events,
when fiction sinks fathom-deep by the side of truth. And
the stern Judgment-Lines start out that bring lies to an end.
A besom of Justice suddenly sweeps the board. In a world
where everything seems tangled, and no truth seems able to
free itself from falsehood—it is staggering to find oneself
face to face with an absolutely clear issue. There is generally

so much truth in every lie—one hardly knows what to do with a lie that is a lie.[1]

The stern Judgment-Lines do not often start out like that. In this world right and wrong, truth and falsehood, do not usually appear as simply contrasted as black and white.

Apart from that pervasive difficulty, the choices open to Z are limited in every direction by his own physical and psychic endowments. He cannot put a telescope to a blind eye if he has not got one, even though that is the very thing that ought to be done in the circumstances. The choices open to him are limited also 'by the purposes, traditions and established habits of the business, trades-union, administrative department or society to which he belongs'.[2] That is to say, Z's choices are further complicated by the fact that to a large extent he has to act as a member of a collective body, and not just as an individual. All the same, it remains true that he is subject to an absolute moral obligation although (mercifully for his pride!) he is not given opportunities of displaying himself as the pure champion of what is absolutely good or absolutely true. It is always and everywhere Z's absolute duty to do his relative best—to do what is best or least bad having regard to all the circumstances that in each case have to be taken into account. When Z is convinced that a certain course of action is God's will for him, however far short of the ideal it may fall, the demand upon him is unconditional. In this sense, and in this sense only, the demands of the Christian ethic are absolute.

It should be added that the rest of us are not in a position to judge how far Z is measuring up to this demand. For Z's relationship to God is not only personal, but private: only God and himself are in a position to know about it and to scrutinize it. It was with regard to this final relationship in which each man stands to God that St Paul said: 'With me it is a very small

---

[1] See *A Forty Years' Friendship*, ed. by S. L. Ollard, p. 130.
[2] *Christian News-Letter* (*C. N. L.*), No. 9 (27th December, 1939).

thing that I should be judged by you or by any human court. I do not even judge myself. . . . It is the Lord who judges me.'[1] Christ himself warned us not to judge how other people stand in this final relationship to God (though of course we may have to judge them in relation to the church or to civil society). 'Judge not', he said, 'that you be not judged.'[2]

The second relationship in which Z stands is that into which he has been brought as a member of the church. The church in this context means the universal community of believers in Christ which is embodied in local and national churches and is at present unhappily split up into denominations. But what I have to say under this head will apply more or less to all of them. The church is the community of those who have been visibly drawn into the coming age while still living in this age. The characteristic activities of the church are the proclamation of the gospel which announces the arrival of the coming age, and the celebration of the sacraments which are the outward and visible signs of its presence.

Z as a churchman has a responsibility for seeing that the work of evangelization and of building up the church everywhere, so that it is light and leaven in the world, is being done and is being well done. This is what I call his ecclesiastical, as distinguished from his political, responsibility. Professional or *ex officio* ecclesiastical responsibility rests upon the ordained ministry. Z might of course be an ordained minister, but it is much more likely that he is a layman and I shall proceed on that assumption. Still as a layman, it is his duty to take an active, and not merely a passive, part in the corporate life, witness and discipline of the church, and this is what most people mean when they talk about the place or function of the laity in the church. That is an important subject, but it is not our subject here. We are concerned with Z's political, not with his ecclesiastical, responsibility.

Nevertheless, there is such a thing as a proper concern of

[1] I Cor. 4.3f.   [2] Matt. 7.1.

the church and of churchmen as such with politics, and Z
ought to know what it is and what it is not. So, although I
am leaving Z's ecclesiastical duties on one side, I shall say
something about the proper and improper modes in which
the church as such and churchmen as such may attempt to
discharge their political responsibilities, and what pitfalls
should be avoided.

The third relationship in which Z always stands is that into
which he entered by his birth into this world or this age, as
distinguished from his rebirth into the church and the age to
come. It embraces all the things and persons and institutions
that exist in the creation and, in Z's case, particularly all those
that impinge directly on his own existence. It includes therefore all the social groups and natural relationships in which by
God's providence and ordinance and the necessities of historical existence Z finds himself—the family and education,
international, national and local politics, industry, agriculture,
commerce, finance, all trades and professions, scientific
research, the arts and in fact all that we have comprised under
the names culture and civilization. In all these spheres or relations, or in so many of them as Z finds himself placed, he is
called to glorify and obey God and to serve his fellowmen. By
'political responsibility' I mean all that.

III

How is Z to know what God wants him to do in this third
area of responsibility which, since he is a layman, ought to
occupy the great bulk of his time and attention? How is he to
vote? In what directions shall he bring to bear such social
influence as he can command? How is he to solve this or that
problem that arises in his business, in his trade union, at the
co-op., at the community centre? Which side, if either, ought
he to take in such and such a public controversy?

We will consider first what the church can and what it
cannot do to guide him in the discharge of these political

H

responsibilities. Broadly speaking, the church can tell Z in a general way what sort of a social order he should be working for, but it cannot tell him precisely what *he* ought to do about it. As has been said: 'there is a marked difference between the question, "what ought to be done about society?" and the question, "what ought I and what can I do about this particular problem of society which my experience and my work thrusts upon my attention?" '[1]

It is the office of the church as such and especially of its ministers—it is the office of mosaic prophecy—to expound the law of God as it is revealed in the Bible, as it has been elucidated in the Christian tradition, and as it bears upon human conduct today. The law of God both in its rudimentary and in its developed forms is a guide to the permanent will of God for mankind but, as we have seen, it does not supply a code of legislation or of precise precepts that are applicable in all times and places. The church's exposition of the law of God ought to inform Z's mind and to keep the great divine imperatives ringing in his ears. It should deepen his insight into the problems that his experience and his work thrust upon him, but it will not as a rule show him exactly what he ought to do. The church is not qualified to lay down the law for him in that sense, still less to issue a party whip.

The Church is not a political party, but it is a pre-political organization. Within the Church people should be able to discover the grounds upon which they make political, and indeed all other, decisions. The Church cannot enter the political firing-line, identifying itself with one political party, forming a party of its own, officially supporting a programme of its own. But it stands at the base: from it men and women derive their conception of justice, mercy, truth; their perception (always partial, always liable to be corrupted by sin) of the things which have to be

[1] *C. N. L.*, No. 285 (14th May, 1947).

fought against and fought for: to it they return for faith renewed and visions re-enlightened.[1]

The church may be able to do all this for Z, but it cannot relieve him of his responsibility for making his own decisions.

One reason why the church as such cannot tell Z what he ought to do in the problems that face him as a banker, or as a docker, or as a town councillor, is that neither the ordained ministry, nor ecclesiastical assemblies or synods, nor his fellow-Christians as such can be expected to possess such a knowledge of the facts of the case as would give the necessary weight to their judgment upon it. As Dr J. H. Oldham has said: 'Where judgment depends on expert knowledge, the Church as a corporate society is not competent to pronounce judgment. The demand that the Church as an ecclesiastical body should keep out of politics is a proper demand, in so far as it means that the clergy, or assemblies mainly guided by the clergy, are not as such competent to dictate policy in political and economic affairs.'[2] However profound their insight into the Christian faith and into the law of God, Z's church and his fellow-churchmen do not know first-hand or from within the facts with which he has got to deal; and in order to decide what he ought to do Z needs not only the deepest possible insight into the *faith* but also the best available understanding of the *facts*.

Politics—and this holds of politics in the broadest sense—is the art of the possible. It is only those who are within an actual situation or who are in a position to comprehend it from within that can know what are the possibilities between which a choice can be made and must be made. It is no good telling a worker that he ought to go on working when his fellow-workmen are coming out on what you think is an unjustified strike, if in fact his particular job cannot be done unless their jobs are being done too. Doctrinaires—and ecclesiastics are not

[1] *C. N. L.*, No. 219 (18th October, 1944).
[2] *C. N. L.*, No. 24 (10th April, 1940).

exempt from the temptation to be doctrinaire—prescribe for imaginary or ideal or wished-for situations instead of for real ones, because their noses have not been rubbed in the actual facts that have got to be dealt with. And the various forms of Christian casuistry which do deal with real possibilities often fail Z at the crucial point of decision. For example, it is easy to say that a university teacher in his free time should get to know his pupils as well as possible and take part in the general activities of the university. It is also his duty to keep abreast of the advances in his subject and his opportunities of doing the most useful service in his job may depend on his devoting all the time he can spare to original research. His problem is how to reconcile these various claims, and no outsider can help him much. Or again, an industrial worker 'may ask, "Is it lawful for men to join a trade union?—to work hard with a view to promotion?—to stand for election to the town council?" On almost any scheme of Christian casuistry the answer to each of these questions, set in general terms, would be "yes". Yet the really critical question is to choose between them. . . . The individual has to discover where "to throw his weight" among the tangled mass of relative goods and evils forming the industrial scene.'[1]

I would even say that ecclesiastical assemblies should as a rule be prevented from passing resolutions about what ought to be done in regard to social, political and economic problems. 'Church bodies meeting in convention (it has been said) often pass resolutions on many, if not most, of the controversial social problems of the time. A sceptical old minister . . . has described this type of transaction as "the most harmless form of amusement which the human mind has ever devised".'[2] But it is not harmless or amusing. The members of ecclesiastical assemblies, whether they are clerics or laymen, are elected or appointed because of their competence in ecclesiastical affairs,

[1] W. G. Symons in *C. N. L.*, No. 124 (11th March, 1942).
[2] W. L. Sperry, *Religion in America*, p. 64.

and it is about those affairs that they are qualified to take decisions and to pass resolutions. They have no special competence to say what anyone ought to do in a trade or profession or department of civil life, where expert technical knowledge of the facts is required.

Political resolutions by ecclesiastical assemblies or political pronouncements by clerics frequently encourage irresponsibility. They give those who pass them or make them or hear them the illusion that, because something has been said and written down and even published, something has been done, or at least that something will be done by somebody, which unfortunately does not follow at all. A witty archbishop once said: 'The clergy have just now a strange mania for signing declarations. I think I could manage to get three-fourths of them to sign a declaration against an eclipse, if I could only persuade them that in some oblique way it expressed some party feeling which they happened to be indulging in at the moment'.[1] I should hope then that, whenever he has the chance, Z will try to prevent ecclesiastics and ecclesiastical assemblies from making pronouncements or passing resolutions on subjects outside their competence—on conditions in the docks, for instance, or on conditions in Pondoland. He should always ask, and ask out loud: 'By this resolution *who precisely* is committing himself to doing *precisely what*?' If, for example, a British ecclesiastical body wants to pass a resolution about the colour bar, he might propose as a rider that everyone who votes for it thereby commits himself to inviting one or more coloured persons in this country to spend next Christmas in his home. Good would be done either way, although it is probable that, if such a criterion were applied, most resolutions of this kind would be dropped.

The dropping of them, if their words are in no jeopardy of being made flesh, is gain, not loss. The truth is not then being obscured that changes are effected in this world and things get

[1] See Macdonell, *Life of Archbishop Magee*, ii, p. 87.

done by individuals or groups of individuals deciding to do what actually lies within their province and their powers. Lamartine said that 'politics should never be put in writing, but enacted in flesh and bone',[1] and one can see what he meant. I am not saying, however, that the church by its writings and utterances can do nothing to help Z to see his political duties. What I am saying is that the church as such has done what it can usefully do when it has given its members the deepest possible understanding of the teaching of the Bible, and has incited and encouraged them to face their political responsibilities for themselves in the light not only of the faith which the Bible enshrines but also of the facts with which they have got to deal.

Nevertheless, there is another way in which the church can, at least indirectly, help lay men and women in the understanding and discharge of their civilian and professional responsibilites, and that is by providing the machinery through which, or the auspices under which, they can meet, and draw together upon the prophetic gift which they share and which can illuminate their technical knowledge of their particular job or problem. The church, since it is not or should not be identified with employers or employed, or with any political party or sectional interest, has the advantage of being able to provide a meeting ground for laymen who would not otherwise be easily brought together into close and friendly communication.

But the church has so far fallen down badly on the help it could give in this field, as compared with what it does to help its members with their ecclesiastical responsibilities. This was forcibly pointed out some years ago by Dr Kathleen Bliss in the following passage:

> What is being done to help the ordinary Christian layman to discover what Christian obedience means for him as

[1] See H. R. Whitehouse, *Life of Lamartine*, i, p. 365.

worker and citizen? Supposing we consider for a moment what is done in our churches to help those who serve the Church as teachers in Sunday Schools. There are books and journals: the Anglicans and the Free Churches have specialists whose sole concern it is to advise and train Sunday School teachers: there are frequent conferences and colleges holding regular courses of training. But what about the man who wants to obey God in his calling as a shop steward? He can find general Christian ethical teaching, and general Christian social teaching, and he gets some moral guidance from the Bible and probably from the pulpit. But if he wants to discover what his Christian obedience should be in the matter of the closed shop, where is he to go? There are no skilled advisers, no regular conferences, and he lacks the means whereby he can get into contact with fellow-Christian shop stewards who share his difficulties.[1]

I suggested at the end of Chapter III that Christians who share particular problems or responsibilities, e.g. in the same industry or on the same local government authority, could form 'prophetic groups', though it would be a mistake to call them that, since it would savour of pretensiousness. The church would be doing a useful work if it did more than it is doing to provide conditions in which such groups could be formed, though of course they do not have to wait upon ecclesiastical encouragement or approval. Divine enlightenment is more likely to come to all of us if we are fertilizing one another's minds and checking one another's judgment than if we are each left to depend on our own individual powers of intellect or intuition. F. D. Maurice said that prophetic wisdom is supernatural 'not because it comes in sudden gusts, in some oracular afflatus, but in proportion as it is toilsome, self-distrusting, open to correction, ready to receive hints and

[1] *C. N. L.*, No. 278 (22nd January, 1947).

illumination from any source'.[1] Where are those conditions more likely to be met than in personal encounter and confidential communication between the members of a well-mixed prophetic group?

This is not just a good idea that has occurred to me as one that would be worthy trying out. Far from it. During the last dozen years or so there has been a spontaneous growth of such groups among lay Christians in various countries. In some countries, such as Holland, Germany, and Sweden, there now exist special institutes or foundations to foster among laymen, whatever their occupation, the exercise of their prophetic gift and calling. These institutes and foundations bear different names and adopt various methods. They are autonomous, but their activities are to some extent co-ordinated by the work of the Ecumenical Institute at Bossey in Switzerland, where meetings are held of international groups of lay people. In Britain we have nothing so impressive to point to as the Evangelical Academies in Germany, but there is a corresponding movement among laymen here, and in the following chapter I shall have something to say about one manifestation of it—the Christian Frontier—with which I happen to be closely acquainted and upon whose experience I can draw.[2]

IV

I will conclude this chapter by asking whether there is not something else that the church could do in order to equip its members to play their part in the running of this world. In its own inner life the church might encourage, where at

[1] F. D. Maurice, *Prophets and Kings*, p. 79.

[2] Other examples in Britain would be William Temple College at Rugby, Christian Action, the Iona Community in Scotland, the Sheffield Industrial Mission, and Kingsgate, Dunford and other colleges founded by the Y.M.C.A. On the analogous developments in Holland, see *C.N.L.*, No. 266 (7th August, 1946); in Germany, see *C.N.L.*, No. 324 (10th November, 1948) and July, 1954, also *The Bridge* (November, 1954), pp. 8-16; in Sweden, see Olov Hartman, *The Sigtuna Foundation* (1955).

present it seems mostly to discourage, the dispositions and qualities of character that will be required in men and women who are going to influence for good those areas of the world in which God places them and who are going to fight against the downward drag of a world centred on itself. In the world, where there is complacency Christians should be agents of disturbance, where there is shoddiness they should be agents of integrity, and where there is timidity they should be fighters. It might be expected that the citizens of the age to come would be more often and more clearly marked by these characteristics than men who regard themselves only as citizens of the present age. But are they? Is it likely that Z, in the course of the ordinary life of the church, will find himself acquiring the dispositions with which he must engage in the struggle to keep the life of this world clean and just and wholesome and always open to improvement?

There is a real difficulty here. It is the proper office of the church to evoke and form in its members towards God a creaturely, docile, obedient, penitent and humble attitude, and towards the neighbour a disposition that is kind, forbearing, helpful and good-natured. And to the church itself with its rich tradition and age-long experience the individual member must always stand related as a disciple towards his teacher. But is it a necessary corrollary of all this that in the worship, government and orientation of the church, especially at the local level, the laity should be as receptive and quiet and uncritical and easy-going as they commonly are, and that the clergy should apparently love to have them so? There is now a long tradition that this should be the case, especially but not only in the Church of Rome. In the last century, Dom Guéranger, the Abbot of Solesmes, said that the laity are 'essentially subject to government, and are radically incapable of exercising any spiritual authority, either directly or by delegation'.[1] Protestants should beware of treating such a

[1] See Congar, *Jalons, etc.*, p. 327. Cp. *supra* pp. 76f.

proposition with superior scorn, for, as Père Congar has remarked, Protestantism whatever its original intentions and ethos is now 'in effect almost as much clericalized' as Roman Catholicism.[1] Are churchgoers on the whole as socially acquiescent as their non-church-going neighbours, and sometimes more so, because the church, and particularly its ministers, have failed to stimulate, and provide scope for, the exercise of certain powerful and dangerous gifts of the Spirit that are not easily reconciled with those mentioned at the beginning of this paragraph? I will give a few illustrations of what I mean by that question.

I said that where there is complacency Christians should be agents of disturbance. Democracy has been defined as a society that tries to give constitutional expression to the asking of awkward questions, though some forms of so-called democracy (near as well as far from home) seem to have just the opposite effect. That would not of course be an adequate definition of the church, but it is certainly a thing that the church ought to do. It may be rash to generalize but my impression is that by and large in the churches the asking of awkward questions is more or less severely frowned upon. Bishop Creighton said that 'the function of a teacher is to be an intellectual mustard plaster',[2] but it does not appear to be the way of the clergy to regard their teaching office in that light. Anyone who causes a bit of friction or who rocks the boat is liable to be looked upon as letting the church down. Is this state of affairs a legacy from the days of the churches' ascendancy and security, or is it a sign of their present weakness and dependence on smooth-running organization, that they cannot now take outspoken criticism within their ranks? Anyhow, churches that stand in need of radical reformation ought to find ways of welcoming disturbers of their peace, and when they do so they will better equip their members to take part in the reformation of the world as well as of the

[1] *Ibid.*, p. 75. [2] Quoted by C. A. Alington, *A Dean's Apology*, p. 38.

122

church. It was a fine, though unintended, tribute that the old lady at the funeral paid to Mr Gladstone, when someone pointed out to her that he was present. 'Oh', she said, 'I do hope he's not come to create a disturbance.'[1]

Again, where there is shoddiness Christians should be agents of integrity. God forbid that churches should fall under the control of intellectual or aesthetic, any more than of social, snobs. But there is little risk of that at present. The 'age of the common man' seems to be working out towards a universal mediocrity, but it has its standards. The church should be expected to surpass them, whereas often it falls below them. In the matter of art, for instance. Why do not inconoclasts arise within the church and throw out those numerous stained-glass windows and church furnishings which are of such deplorable quality that we would not tolerate them for a moment in our private houses? Or in the matter of music and of public reading and speaking and of printing. With bright exceptions, the church is not at pains to see that these things are all done as well as they possibly can be done, and it is much too easily pleased with second-rate and third-rate achievements. It seems to be supposed that, if the works of the present age are done within the context of the age to come, all kinds of incompetent performance can be excused, like the man who conducted the band of a temperance society and, when someone complained that the music was excruciating, replied, 'I know they are not good musicians, but they are such good teetotallers!' A church that acquiesces in shoddiness even in its sanctuaries is not likely to send people out into the world bent on raising standards everywhere and on seeing that everything, however 'secular', is offered to God as perfectly as possible.

Once more, where there is timidity Christians should be fighters. In the world the service of Christ's cause often requires a man to fight against heavy odds and to say No to

[1] See *The Listener*, 28th June, 1951, p. 1031.

all the yes-men. In 1946 the following paragraph appeared in *The Christian News-Letter*:

It is by the courageous action of individuals much more than by resolutions of religious bodies that changes for good can be brought about in public affairs. It has come to our knowledge that one of our readers who is a director of a company protested strongly at a meeting of the Board when it was proposed to declare a dividend of thirty per cent. His colleagues seemed to think that he was mad. Why should not the shareholders take thirty per cent. out of the business if they wanted to? The company in question pays low wages and has no pension scheme and no sickness benefit. The motion to reduce the dividend received no support. But the Christian battle is a never-ending struggle and success or failure in one round is neither here nor there. The point is that opportunities for the Christian conscience to assert itself are ready to hand for those who have eyes to see, and the courage to seize them.[1]

But is life in the church, as it is, calculated to give men insight and courage like that? Or, to put the question the other way round, do men who are fighting that sort of battle in the world receive the support and fellowship that the church should give them? Père Congar quotes this authentic piece of testimony about a Catholic layman:

I have just seen X. He is certainly one of the most capable and influential trade unionists. He has just had to retire at the age of 45 in lamentable circumstances. 'For twenty years', he said to me, 'except at C. with F. T., I have always had to fight alone. When I was wrong, as sometimes I certainly was, no one really helped me to see clearly. When I was right, no one has supported me in my struggle.'[2]

[1] *C.N.L.*, No. 265 (24th July, 1946).   [2] Congar, *op. cit.*, p. 620.

Does an ordinary Christian congregation give its own members, let alone outsiders, the sense that here is a company of people who are engaged in a struggle and who are supporting one another in the fight each is engaged in at his allotted station in the world? It was well said of Tom Paine that he

> with his harsh earnestness, his daring if unlettered mind, his championship of common folk, and his life of self-forgetful adventure seems far nearer in spirit to the Christ whom he denied, than the comfortable gentlemen who, with more dignity and learning but with less of love and sacrifice, wrote tracts under such stimulating titles as *A Layman's Protest against the Profane Blasphemy, false Charges, and illiberal Invective of Thomas Paine*.[1]

There is nowadays, thank God, a growing number of Christian congregations of which it can be said that they do consist of comrades who are supporting one another in an adventurous struggle; but are they not still quite exceptional? It is true that Z must be prepared 'to accept loneliness for a bride and to cultivate fortitude upon a rock': he must be prepared, if necessary, to fight by himself with his trust in God alone. But it is not God's will that men should have to struggle in such loneliness, where it can be remedied. It is the calling of the church, and of every local church, to be the place where Christ's people are together in the forefront of the battle both *for* this world and *against* it. In so far as the church is not at present responsive to that calling in its normal institutional life, there is all the more reason why opportunities should be made for Christians and kindred spirits to stand by one another in groups, specially constituted for that purpose.

[1] See C. E. Padwick, *Henry Martyn*, p. 49.

VI

Frontier Methods and Maxims

I

IT is only within the last fifteen years or so that the word
'frontier' has acquired a special meaning in the vocabu-
lary of Christians. It is used now to indicate the non-
ecclesiastical areas of the common life, in which laymen
naturally spend most of their time, in which most of their
moral and human problems arise, but in which it is not the
province of the church to tell them exactly what they ought
to do. One day the origins of this use of the word may be
made the subject of a piece of academic research. It is, to say
the least, convenient to have a word that points to those ranges
of duty which are not subject to the control or direct guidance
of the church as an organized institution but are none the less
of paramount importance if God's will is to be done on earth
as it is in heaven. If it is true, as we have suggested, that the
nature of the Christian concern with the affairs of this world
has hitherto been insufficiently explored, then it is a promising
sign that the word 'frontier' has been brought into service to
fasten attention on it. The frontier, in this sense, is a common
concern of all Christians, to whatever church they belong or
however loosely they are attached to any church at all. If there
are differences of approach to problems that arise on the frontier, they cut across the lines of ecclesiastical allegiance. In this
sphere, therefore, it is found that close co-operation between
Christians is possible on an ecumenical basis.

I am going in this chapter, first, to say a little about the

126

Christian Frontier Council and its methods of working and, then, at greater length to frame and illustrate for Z's benefit some maxims about politics which to my mind are the outcome of frontier experience and reflection. I want to emphasize that the Christian Frontier Council lays no claim whatever to a monopoly of the frontier idea nor to the use of frontier methods, which are in fact being used by many other Christian groups that are seeking prophetic insight into their social and political responsibilities.

II

It was in 1942, through the initiative of Dr J. H. Oldham and under the auspices, though not under the control, of the British Council of Churches, that there came into existence a body known as the Christian Frontier Council.[1] In itself it was and has remained quite a small body of lay people who occupy a variety of positions of responsibility in public life, mostly in London. Its activities have always been restricted by limitations of staff and resources. The Council holds regular evening meetings when, together with specially invited guests, the members not only consider together some frontier subject but worship and have a meal together. At least once a year they spend a weekend in conference. The Council has, not inaptly, been described as an experiment in the possibilities of friendship in which, through free intercourse, minds stimulate, quicken, and enrich one another.

In addition to its own activities, the Council sponsors the formation of special groups which undertake to face the question of Christian responsibility for what is happening in particular areas of the national life. Such frontier groups follow more or less the same methods of meeting and working as the Council itself, but their concentration on whatever inquiry

[1] A leaflet about the work of the Christian Frontier Council can be had if a stamped and addressed envelope is sent to the Secretary, 8 The Cloisters, Windsor Castle.

they take in hand is both more expert and more intense. Further, the publications which the Council has sponsored[1] have made available for all who were interested any conclusions that had been reached; its publications have also served as a link with other similar groups that have been started independently and as a bond with individual Christians who have been contending in isolation with frontier problems. In order to illustrate the working of frontier groups, I will mention three, none of which is political in the narrower sense of the word.

Sir Walter Moberly's book *The Crisis in the University* (1949), as he explained in the preface, was the outcome of the work of a frontier group, the members of which were drawn from the teaching staffs of universities in Great Britain. For several years they had been meeting in private conference to discuss what were the responsibilities of Christians in the contemporary university world. After preparing and scrutinizing a number of documents, some of which were published,[2] they reached a point at which they asked one of their number to write a book that would give expression to their findings or at least to the questions on which they wanted to focus attention. The matter did not end there, for *The Crisis in the University* made so considerable a stir in the academic world that in most, if not in all, of the British universities local groups of dons and others were formed to discuss the questions that had been raised with special reference to their own immediate problems and tasks. The ferment that was thus begun is still working.[3]

---

[1] In addition to sponsoring the publication of books, the Council has had a regular organ in *The Christian News-Letter*, which was published weekly or fortnightly from 1939 to 1949, *The Frontier*, which was published monthly from 1950 to 1952, and *Christian News-Letter*, which has been published quarterly since 1953.

[2] A series of twelve 'University Pamphlets' that were published by the S.C.M. Press in 1946.

[3] There is a co-ordinating body known as the 'Dons' Advisory Group', which arranges periodical conferences, etc. (Address: Annandale, North End Road, London, N.W.11.)

This is a good example of the results that may follow from the initiation and initiative of one frontier group.

A second example is the work of a frontier group of doctors (Protestant and Roman Catholic) who met regularly in London for some years to consider from a Christian point of view the human and ethical problems that arise in their profession but that tend to be put in the shade by questions of technical skill and scientific discovery. This group also eventually produced a book, entitled *The Doctor's Profession* (1949), and edited by the Rev. Daniel Jenkins who was at that time a member of the staff of the Christian Frontier Council and who had contributed to the deliberations of the group in his capacity as a theologian. A theologian or two, by the way, can make useful contributions to the work of specialized or professional frontier groups, provided they are ready to listen and to learn as well as to talk, and provided they do not insist on how the questions should be framed, which is what theologians like to do. In this connexion some words once written by Dr Oldham are worth recalling:

> In conferences which consider the relation of the Christian faith to society, the initiative generally lies with the clergy, and they tend almost inevitably to bring the whole discussion within the framework of their own specifically religious approach. The problems which the layman experiences do not get on to the agenda. We shall never come to real grips with the relation of Christian faith to modern society until we recognise the existence of this clerical perspective and refuse to allow it to dominate the discussion.[1]

Frontier methods are designed to obviate that danger; but it is still necessary to take care that the clerical perspective having been expelled through the front door does not return through the back door, since clerics if admitted at all are usually more

[1] *C.N.L.*, No. 59 (11th December, 1940).

talkative, if not more articulate, than laymen. Theology itself will become more relevant and more meaningful if it has to speak to the real problems that laymen encounter in their jobs. It has been said of theological students (and the same might be said of some theologians) that, when faced with political problems needing hard thought, they 'quit grappling with the here and now and take an elevator up to the eternal, where refuge can be found in theological platitudes'.[1]

A third example is a group of educationalists who combined to examine what factors in the national system of education are favourable and what factors are unfavourable to Christian faith and practice. After a broad survey of the question, they invited a number of Christian headmasters and headmistresses from different types of secondary school to give evidence and to describe how they were trying to make the Christian faith a living reality in their own schools. These pieces of first-hand testimony were felt to be so full of interest and encouragement that it was decided to publish a selection of them in book form. The book appeared in 1954 and was edited by Professor W. O. Lester Smith under the title, *The School as a Christian Community*.

These examples, which could be multiplied, show that there is a variety of ways in which a frontier group can set about its task. What is essential is that the persons who are invited to join a group shall have as expert as possible an understanding of the subject that is being investigated, which may mean that they will not be those who are the most enthusiastic or the most devout! It is also essential that the members of a frontier group shall meet in conditions in which they come to trust one another as friends, however much they differ in opinions. The frontier group method can be extended into every area of the common life, and it can be operated at all levels from the shop floor to the top stories in Whitehall.

[1] *C.N.L.*, No. 303 (21st January, 1948).

III

The odds are against Z's being a don, a medical practitioner or a schoolteacher, but whatever his own occupation may be, and in addition to what he can do about that, he has as a citizen responsibility for what goes on in the field of politics in the narrower sense, that is, in local, national and international government. While it would be ridiculous to say that every Christian ought to try to take a direct part in government by entering the civil service or by becoming a candidate for political office, it is not ridiculous to say that in a country like Great Britain today, where government formally rests and depends on the consent of the governed, every Christian ought to try to cultivate political wisdom and to keep a watching brief on the proceedings of those who are in positions of authority.

We must of course beware of taking it for granted (as the British are much tempted to do) that the system of government that has come to prevail in our own country ought to prevail or is suitable for export everywhere. For instance, we often now make the mistake of assuming that the universal adult franchise is a *sine qua non* of good government. The best possible form of government in any particular country in any particular period will correspond to the peculiarities of its history and the stage of development it has reached. Whilst we should be on our guard against people who have a facility in the utterance of political generalizations, still people with the appropriate gifts and opportunities may with advantage to us all study the nature of government the world over and try to show what are in general the criteria of good government and bad.[1] But the kind of political wisdom which Z, being a Christian in Britain, ought especially to cultivate is that which will enable him to act responsibly with regard to the government of his own country.

[1] This task has lately been essayed under the auspices of the World Council of Churches: see *Social Questions—The Responsible Society in a World Perspective* (an Evanston Survey).

I am going therefore to adumbrate, for Z's benefit, some maxims which I believe to have a practical bearing on political conditions in this country. These maxims are not merely the product of reflection on my own limited political experience. Though I am alone responsible for the way they are framed and illustrated, they have to a large extent been arrived at by frontier methods. I am assuming that Z, if he was not previously convinced, is convinced now that God wills him to bear his share of responsibility for the government and conduct of this world, and also that God wills this world to be governed in accordance with the necessities and potentialities of this world or of this age. That is to say, Z understands that he does not have to contract out of politics because in politics the ideal possibilities of the age to come cannot be realized.

(i) My first maxim, then, is that Z will be *realistic about the starting-point of political action*. He will start from where he is. It might be thought that is obvious. But in the modern period Christians have been almost as much inclined as secular romantics and idealists to found their politics on the unacknowledged assumption that they were living either in a state of the world that is past beyond recall (e.g. the middle ages, the *ancien régime*, or the age of *laissez faire*) or in a state of the world that has not yet been realized and perhaps never will be realized (utopianism). Those are two forms of historical absenteeism. It is the will of God that we should serve him and our neighbours politically, as otherwise, in the actual, given, historical contingencies in which we find ourselves, however disagreeable they may appear to us or however much we feel we should like to be living in another period. As Sir Robert Peel wrote to Mr Croker in 1842: 'If you had to constitute new societies, you might on moral and social grounds prefer cornfields to cotton factories, an agricultural to a manufacturing population. But our lot is cast, and we cannot recede.'[1]

Dr Oldham made the same point in *The Christian News-Letter*:

[1] C. S. Parker, *Life of Sir Robert Peel*, ii, p. 529.

There is no cutting ourselves out from the stream of history and re-entering it at some future date.[1]

And again:

What is unprofitable is to waste valuable time in framing schemes for an imaginary world instead of changing a bit of the real world by altering the decisions and acts that are within our immediate control. . . .

. . . It is not given to us mortals to lift ourselves out of the struggle of human existence and from a detached vantage-point create a pattern of what society ought to be. That is God's affair. To us is given a humbler but heroic task—to recognise untruth and denounce it; to see evil and attack it; to perceive what is wrong and find out the means of setting it right.[2]

I would add that Z should not only look for evils to be denounced and put right in the world as he finds it; he should also be on the look out for good, the *hidden* work or presence of Christ, that may be unacknowledged because it appears in a novel garb or bears an unchristian label.

As Z reflects upon his political duty, he will be on his guard against propositions that begin with, or imply, an 'if only . . .' clause. 'If only . . .' is the hall-mark of escapism in politics as in one's personal life. Dostoevsky makes one of his characters say:

'If only it were not for these people, if only it were not for these circumstances, if only he could fly away from this accursed place—he would be altogether regenerated, would enter on a new path. That was what he believed in, and what he was yearning for.'[3]

[1] *C.N.L.*, No. 22 (27th March, 1940).
[2] *C.N.L.*, No. 57 (27th November, 1940).
[3] Dostoevsky, *The Brothers Karamazov* (Ev. Ed.), ii, 3.

That, emphatically, is what Z will *not* believe in. It is on the basis of 'whereas . . .' and 'given that . . .' clauses that he will determine his duty. For example, in Britain in 1956 Z will not waste time indulging in nostalgic laments for 'the good old days' or in tedious recollection of 'the bad old days', but will accept the 'Welfare State' as his starting-point, will acknowledge what is good in it, and then will look out for ways in which it can be improved, for perils latent in it that can be averted, and for corruptions to which it is prone that can be cured.[1]

(ii) Secondly, Z will be *realistic about the methods by which things have to be done in politics*. In a dictatorship there is very little that can be done politically by anyone unless he belongs to the faction in power—except to conspire for its overthrow, and that has become practically impossible with the elaboration of totalitarian techniques by the dictators. But in a free society it is happily otherwise. The freedom of our society does not however mean that it must be left to each individual citizen by his own individual action to try to improve the lot of himself and (if he is altruistic) of other people just as and when he likes. In a society whose structure and economy are as complicated as ours, the way to secure justice for ourselves and to do justice to our fellow-citizens must be to a large extent by collective action. Private charity can supplement it, but cannot take its place. As *The Christian News-Letter* said in 1940:

The only way in which, in the organised life of society, desirable changes can be brought about, and undesirable changes prevented, is by political action. All talk about a better society is idle day-dreaming till it is translated into public policy. To suppose that we can meet the needs of other men today by individual action, except within a very

[1] See my article on 'The Welfare State from a Christian point of view' in *Theology*, December, 1952.

restricted field, is to be blind to the nature of modern society.[1]

And we must at once go further and say that in this country political action as a rule means party political action. Z must be realistic about party politics. Some Christians excuse themselves from engaging in politics altogether because it means taking part in the rough and tumble and the somewhat dubious proceedings of the party struggle. Here discrimination is called for. There are no parties in the age to come, and for that reason there should be no parties in the church whose characteristic office is to witness to the age to come: St Paul has left us in no doubt about that (see I Corinthians). But in this age and in the government of this world parties have a necessary function to perform. For one thing, they are inevitable because in politics there is always a struggle of contending interests, and it is better that these should be open and organized than covert and without recognizable means of operation. Moreover, parties prevent the monopolizing of power by any one interest or faction. The maintenance of H. M. Opposition together with H. M. Government is a preservative of a free society.

At the same time, Z may well have an uneasy conscience about party politics. In the first place, they afford plenty of evidence of human irrationality. In the biography of Lord Oxford and Asquith the observation is made that the course and fortunes of the movement for Irish Home Rule were determined by circumstances entirely unrelated to its merits. 'The cause of Home Rule was powerfully advanced by proof that Mr Parnell had not been guilty of condoning a murder, and sustained a crucial set-back from the discovery that he had been guilty of living with a married woman'.[2]

But the party political struggle has worse features than its

[1] *C.N.L.*, No. 10 (3rd January, 1940).

[2] Spender and Asquith, *Life of Lord Oxford and Asquith*, i, p. 36.

frequent irrationality. It offers wide scope for the display of man's individual and collective egotism. A man will do for his party what he would not dream of doing for himself, and without any sense of shame. Political parties represent themselves as standing for certain ideals, and this moral or rational element in the construction of parties is important, though politicians are always tempted to exaggerate it. But to succeed or to accomplish anything parties must be engines of interests as well as of ideals, and they must get into power. There would be no sense in being in politics if you disabled yourself from the outset from ever getting into power. The struggle for power is as essential to party politics as the war of ideas.

Z must be realistic about the necessary place and function of power in this age. Luther said that 'he who wants to be a ruler, must have the Devil for his godfather'.[1] 'A right good man may be a very unfit magistrate', said Hooker.[2] Even Talleyrand's cynical remark that 'to make a good Secretary of State at Rome, it is well to choose a bad Cardinal',[3] is one that a wise Christian like Z will not despise. But Dr Oldham made the point more lucidly, if less epigrammatically, when he wrote in *The Christian News-Letter*:

Reforms in the political sphere have never been brought about by idealistic and altruistic impulses alone. Political reforms become possible only when moral forces are to some extent reinforced by material and selfish interests. That is because power and material interest belong to the warp and woof of politics; if it was otherwise, the political sphere would have been transformed into the Kingdom of God. . . . The price of refusing to take account of the realities of politics is to remain impotent in the political field. A statesman who wants to carry a public measure has to appeal,

[1] Quoted by E. G. Rupp, *The Righteousness of God*, p. 305.
[2] R. Hooker, *Works*, ed. J. Keble, iii, p. 306.
[3] See Comte de Saint-Aulaire, *Talleyrand*, p. 35.

136

consciously or unconsciously, to a variety of motives. As a Christian he may be actuated by the noblest spiritual purpose; as a Christian statesman he has to consider what forces in a very mixed society can be rallied to the support of the measure he wishes to carry.[1]

What is true of a Christian statesman is true, *mutatis mutandis*, of any Christian citizen. Z will not expect too much of institutions or of statesmen. He will allow for the fact that the government and the running of this world often necessitate attitudes and actions that would be justly condemned in the government of the church and still more in men's personal relations with one another in their families and their friendships. If Z is hard up, he will not expect to be treated with the same generosity by the tax inspector or by his bank manager as by his father or by his best friend. As Julia Wedgwood said, 'the virtue of political life is justice. Generosity belongs to individual relation.'[2] And political justice has not seldom to be pretty rough justice.

Again, in politics, as in commerce, a man must press his own claims, and a candidate for office must advertise his own competence. A statesman may have to vote for, and even with an air of conviction to defend, policies to which he is opposed —and which in fact he has opposed in cabinet or in the councils of his party—because he is satisfied that even more harm would be done if he broke up his party, and if the aggregate of good it could accomplish were lost. In 1883 when Sir Charles Dilke had refused to vote with his party on the issue of the women's franchise, he wrote in his diary: 'Hartington is very angry with me for not voting, and wants me turned out for it. He has to vote every day for things which he strongly disapproves',[3] i.e. in order to keep the Whigs and the Radicals together in Mr

---

[1] *C.N.L.*, No. 52 (23rd October, 1940).
[2] Julia Wedgwood, *Nineteenth Century Teachers*, p. 295.
[3] Gwynn and Tuckwell, *The Life of Sir Charles W. Dilke*, ii, p. 8.

Gladstone's Liberal cabinet. A statesman may in public have to conceal the truth in a manner which, if followed in his private relationships, would lose him all his friends. Another entry in Dilke's diary (June, 1885) reveals Mr Gladstone himself in a compromising situation:

> It passes my understanding . . . how Mr Gladstone is able to pronounce, as he has done, 'unfounded' the statement that the Cabinet was at odds upon the Irish question at the moment of its defeat. Three of us had resigned on it, and our letters were in his pocket.[1]

A statesman has sometimes to jettison an important, if not essential, moral standard for the sake of a greater good. In politics we ought to hold that treaties and constitutions must be observed—*pacta sunt servanda*—but, as Victor Hugo said, '*il faut quelquefois violer les chartes pour leur faire des enfants*'.[2]

Once more, in politics issues have often to be simplified and ideas popularized in a way that must distress a sensitive conscience and an informed mind. F. S. Oliver said that 'a very nimble and wide-ranging intelligence is usually an obstacle to effective action in practical affairs'.[3] 'The multitude loves to be addressed in tones loud and positive', wrote Wilfrid Ward. 'Well-balanced thought ever seems to it a shadow. Strong statements mean strength: guarded statements, weakness.'[4] A Christian statesman is not required to go around making speeches that are a parade of weakness. He had better come to terms with the fact that, as Mr Christopher Hollis has said, 'the most high-minded of politicians has inevitably to spend a good deal of his time enunciating what he knows to be half-truths—concealing the deficiencies of colleagues and supporting measures of whose desirability he is not wholly

[1] *Ibid.*, ii, 145.　　　　[2] I cannot trace the source of this quotation.
[3] F. S. Oliver, *The Endless Adventure*, ii, 55.
[4] Wilfrid Ward, *Ten Personal Studies*, p. 4.

convinced. There is no other method of team-work possible.'[1]

At the same time, he would be a bad statesman who allowed his own mind to be coarsened and corrupted by the necessities of simplification and of enunciating half-truths. He need not do so. Ernest Thurtle wrote in his autobiography:

In political battles issues have to be simplified, and, for people living in the controversies of the day, philosophical and intellectual qualifications are not practical politics. For that reason it has not been my custom to introduce such qualifications into my political affirmations; *yet they have never been absent from my mind.*[2]

So, on the other hand, Z must not expect too little of the institutions, and of the statesmen, of this age. While he knows that politics can never be completely moralized, and that high-sounding sentiments on the lips of statesmen are often hypocritical, yet he also knows that there is no exact limit to the extent to which politics can be moralized or to which this age can be penetrated by the age to come. He will be a realist, but he will beware of cynicism, machiavellianism, and mere *raisons d'état.* There is, as Croce said,[3] a difference between a 'moral' and a 'moralistic' view of politics. A frontier group dealt with this point some years ago in a paper on 'The Temptations of a Politician'.

The politician in the exercise of his responsibilities is a moral person, and according to his moral stature and moral insight he will, among the choices open to him, prefer one course of action to another. But he cannot lift himself out of the conditions in which he has to act. For this reason . . . we have to distinguish between a moral and a 'moralistic'

[1] *The Tablet*, 7th May, 1955, p. 444.
[2] E. Thurtle, *Time's Winged Chariot*, p. 29 (italics mine).
[3] Benedetto Croce, *Politics and Morals*, pp. 69f.

view of history and judgment of political action. We cannot apply to political decisions copy-book maxims which leave out of account the infinite complexity of the factors which govern concrete action. A truly moral judgment of political action seeks to understand the whole historical situation in which it takes place and asks whether the statesman in making his decision has responded adequately and at the highest level open to him to the demands and necessities of the total situation confronting him. The famous slogan of the militant Nonconformist Conscience that 'what is morally wrong can never be politically right' was fully justified in insisting that no sphere of human life is outside the control of moral obligation but gravely misleading in its too simple and inelastic understanding of moral behaviour in politics.[1]

(iii) Thirdly—and this is a corrollary of the point just made—Z will *not talk much about 'Christian principles'*. I do not myself find it necessary to use that expression at all. It is not an expression that will be found in the Bible; I suspect that it has come into use only in modern times. It is open to various objections. We are seldom told what precisely are the 'Christian principles' to which reference is being made. 'We talk so much of Christian principles', wrote Dom Theodore Wesseling. 'But one rarely hears more than vague general terms, and the Christian principles are rarely enumerated, let alone examined. When it comes to more precision, each one speaks his own mind and his own language.'[2]

When people talk about 'Christian principles', they may have in mind some vague or general propositions about the

[1] *C.N.L.*, No. 277 (8th January, 1947).

[2] Theodore Wesseling, *The Cleansing of the Temple*, pp. 61f. Cp. the Duke of Wellington's saying: 'We hear a great deal of whig principles, and tory principles, and liberal principles, and Mr Canning's principles; but I confess that I have never seen a definition of any of them, and I cannot make to myself a clear idea of what any of them are.' Quoted by Hearnshaw, *Conservatism in England*, p. 187.

value of human personality or the equality of all men in the sight of God, about which all Christians are agreed. But such 'principles' do not get us anywhere because the problem in politics is how to realize them and about that Christians may reasonably disagree. Or by 'Christian principles' there may be meant certain specific policies, such as 'one man, one vote', which are rightly or wrongly favoured by those who use the term, but which are neither 'Christian' nor 'principles'.[1] Talk about 'principles' is sometimes even less creditable than that. 'What people call their principles', said Leslie Stephen, 'are really their pretexts for acting in the obviously convenient way.'[2]

Another objection to talk about 'Christian principles' by either Conservative or Labour politicians is that it carries with it the implication that the cause of their own party is Christian and of the opposing party unchristian, whereas Christians can be equally justified in belonging to either party, and the policy of neither should be identified with the gospel or the church. For this reason the formation of so-called 'Christian political parties' is still more objectionable, and we can be thankful that we are free from them in this country. As for clerical parties, they would be most objectionable of all. Dr Figgis spoke of 'the cardinal error of all clericalist parties in arguing that their decisions, being concerned with religious matters, were of a radically different order from those of other men'.[3]

Talk about 'Christian principles' or indeed any sort of 'principles' also fosters the notion that in any controversy you have only to unearth the 'principle' at stake and then you will know which side you ought to take. But anyone who is capable of analysing what is at stake in most political controversies will perceive that there is more than one principle at stake and that unfortunately they point in different directions. Some words written by Dr Oldham in *The Christian News-Letter*

[1] Cp. E. Barker and R. H. Preston, *Christians in Society*, pp. 82-97.
[2] See J. Morley, *Recollections* (1921 ed.), i, p. 112.
[3] See *Journal of Theological Studies*, 1901, pp. 86f.

with regard to the resistance movement in France during the war may be strong meat for Christians in Britain now, but they strike at the root of the matter:

The will of God to be done in one set of circumstances may be quite different from the fulfilment of his will that is demanded in other circumstances. A man who, in obedience to God's call, commits himself to a public career may in fulfilling his vocation have to perform actions which in another situation would be wrong, but which in the context in which he has to act can only be avoided by renouncing his original decision and withdrawing from the fight in the public sphere. The moral conflict may reach the point at which he feels it right, in political life, to resign his office, in the underground struggle presumably to accept martyrdom. But so long as he adheres to his original course, his particular acts, which are dictated by the unyielding necessities of the actual situation, take their meaning from his fundamental and total choice.

This may at first sight look like the vicious doctrine that the end justifies the means, which can lead to every kind of fanaticism and crime. It is, in fact, totally different. But it can easily degenerate into the other as soon as we substitute abstract moral principles and ends for the living, daily response to the renewed demands of a God whose character and purpose do not change, or too lightly identify his purpose with our own limited and darkened understanding of it.[1]

We rightly admire and commend what we call 'a man of principle' in contrast to an opportunist, or to a time-server, but then by a man of principle we mean a man in whose ears the great divine imperatives are ever ringing—a man who has a sense of absolute or unconditional moral obligation (see *supra*, p. 111), not a man who supposes he has got his duties

[1] *C.N.L.*, No. 205 (5th April, 1944).

neatly tabulated and fixed in a set of abstract principles. Anyhow, Z's final loyalty in politics as elsewhere will be not to principles but to the living God who makes his will known to him day by day in each situation as it arises. Dietrich Bonhoeffer said that 'the Christian cannot see his life as a series of principles, but only in its relation to the living God';[1] and Oswald Chambers put the case even more strongly: 'In the final issue Christian principles are found to be antichrist, i.e. an authority other than Christ himself'.[2] Z sees what they meant.

(iv) Fourthly, Z will be *humble enough to work his way up from the bottom.* In politics he will be ready to start as an office boy or on what corresponds to the shop floor; he will not expect to be elevated right away to the managerial staff or to the rank of expert consultant. Some Christians imagine that they should be listened to just because they are Christians, irrespective of whether they have any real knowledge of what is under consideration. It has been well said that 'when Christians turn their attention to the problems of the secular world they must do so clearly understanding that they have to get into the game and humbly and faithfully play their part in it, without claiming peculiar knowledge about secular affairs which enables them to give advice from a superior vantage point above the struggle.'[3]

Let us suppose that Z, though a mature adult in other respects, has only just woken up to the fact of his political responsibilities as a Christian citizen. How and where will he set about educating himself? No doubt he can learn much through studying and discussing national and international politics, but to stop there, or even to start there, is irresponsible. He should begin by taking an interest in local politics, i.e. in the government of the locality in which he is set. He can exercise

[1] D. Bonhoeffer, *Temptation*, p. 11.
[2] Oswald Chambers, *Conformed to His Image*, p. 29.
[3] *C.N.L.*, No. 297 (29th October, 1947).

his right as a citizen and go and listen to meetings of the town or city council. He can obtain the latest report of the Medical Officer of Health, to which every ratepayer is entitled. He can ascertain what is being done about housing and schooling in his neighbourhood. He can attend political meetings and find out for what policies each party stands. Before long he should be able to decide which party to join. That in itself will mark an important step forward in his education. Some years ago a married woman bore this testimony in print:

> It is no use saying that party politics are dirty and accepting without question the benefits they confer; that is to soil our hands far more than to work in the political machine. I speak feelingly, because for years I combined a willingness to discuss politics with a quite abysmal ignorance as to what they were really about. In three years within a local party I have learnt more about how the life of this country is organized than I ever did in the couple of decades since I left school. I have been fascinated by what can be done for a local community by a vigorous party machine, and by the way in which, through its M.P., it can make a real contribution even to national affairs.[1]

Anyone joining a political party with a readiness to be an active member can be sure of a welcome and of an opportunity to do a job of work. 'Office in the local branch of a party is often easy enough to obtain by anyone of reasonable competence who is prepared to do the drudgery it entails and such posts are often stepping-stones to real political influence. Whatever may be true of the top there is plenty of room at the bottom in politics and the bottom is the place to make a start.'[2]

(v) My fifth maxim is that, however far Z goes in his party —even if, perhaps especially if, he were to end up in Downing

[1] Moira Symons on 'Home and Community' in *C.N.L.*, No. 303 (21st January, 1948).

[2] *C.N.L.*, No. 270 (2nd October, 1946).

Street—he will be *both a good party man and a bad party man*. He recognizes that things get done in politics by men combining and working together in parties, and not by a riot of individuals each with his own bright ideas. However, I have already said enough to show why Z will be a *good* party man.

But he will also be a bad party man.[1] He may not give his complete allegiance to any party, for God alone is entitled to receive that. He may not suppose that any party is a hundred per cent. right; he realizes that by definition it represents partial (and not national or universal) interests and ideals, whatever its orators may say during elections. Moreover, Z is liable to have to say: 'This bit of propaganda may appear to be very much in the interests of our party, but it is not true, and therefore I stand out at this point'; or 'This manœuvre may be very clever, and it might get our party into power, but it is dishonest and unscrupulous, and I refuse to have anything to do with it.' Again, Z is aware that parties tend to go on standing for policies which were relevant once, and repeating shibboleths which were apposite once, but which have now become obsolete, and so he may have to abandon a party which is clinging to the past, and the most 'progressive' party is prone to do that in the end.

What some people mean by 'a good party man' is a bigoted partisan, and that Z should never be. He should indeed throw himself into party campaigns with vigour and loyalty to his colleagues, but in the back of his mind he will know that men may be campaigning on the other side with equal sincerity and very likely with equally good reason, and from time to time this knowledge will creep out into the front of his mind and slip out in his speeches. This can be illustrated with regard to the two major parties in Britain today.

During the second world war a frontier group of party politicians considered the question of party allegiance and as an

---

[1] This paragraph is for the most part reproduced from my book, *Good News for Mankind*, p. 72.

outcome of their discussions produced a document entitled *Christians in Politics: Christian Conservatism and Christian Radicalism*,[1] which I shall lay under charge in what follows. This group started by recognizing that 'party allegiances spring from certain fundamental attitudes'—the right and the left, or conservative and radical. At their worst these two attitudes breed on the one hand 'the inertia of uncritical reaction'[2] and on the other 'the cocksure self-righteousness of aggressive progressivism'. But Christians in both parties should see to it that conservatism and radicalism are kept true to their best insights. Then it will be evident that 'both are necessary to fruitful political development'.

For example, conservatives at their best are concerned to see that government 'allows scope for those forms of natural association, such as the family, whose maintenance in relative independence of the state and healthy functioning are necessary to enable men to live as God intended them to live.' The Christian conservative, because he believes that God is at work in history has 'a strong respect for tradition and continuity in national life'. He realizes 'that a just social order cannot be built in a day and that wisdom was not born with him. . . . It will be his concern that freedom shall not be sacrificed to the modern passion for equality, and that carefully built-up traditions and institutions which have come down to us from the past shall not be carelessly destroyed because they do not fulfil the specifications of particular planners at the moment.'[3]

The Christian radical on the other hand is keenly sensitive to the extent of the evil and injustice in the world and to the

[1] *C.N.L.*, No. 263 (26th June, 1946).

[2] Henry Sidgwick said in 1869 'The fact is there is no real conservatism anywhere among educated men. Only *vis inertiae.*' *Memoir of Henry Sidgwick*, p. 196.

[3] P. T. Forsyth's words in *The Principle of Authority* (p. 305) are worth recalling: 'None should depart from tradition but those to whom it is dear. None should be entrusted with the destruction of the past but those who loved it.'

fact that it must be fought. 'To establish justice will often demand radical action, the breaking down of firmly established social orders and forcing through sweeping changes in the face of bitter opposition.' 'An adequate politics is possible', Dr Reinhold Niebuhr has written, 'only if the task of achieving some kind of decent harmony in social relations is essayed with a clear understanding of the stubborn inertia which every social purpose meets in the egoism of individuals and groups.'[1] Tradition may have great virtues but too great a respect for tradition may be a grave handicap to a people. It has been said of the Greeks that 'their chief strength . . . lay in their freedom from hampering intellectual tradition. They had no venerated classics, no holy books, no dead languages to master, no authorities to check their free speculation.'[2]

Whereas conservatives are temperamentally contented with what is or what was, radicals are temperamentally discontented. J. S. Mill said, though doubtless with considerable exaggeration, that 'nothing is more certain than that improvement in human affairs is wholly the work of the uncontented characters'.[3] Finally as regards the present time, the Christian radical seems to realize more candidly than the Christian conservative that 'the question before us today is not whether we shall have a planned society but what kind of a planned society we shall have'.

The Christian then 'will recognize the relativity of party divisions. He will see that there is point in both a responsible conservative and in a responsible radical position.' Beneath their divisions and their rivalry Christians in both parties are at one in wanting society to be ordered in accordance with God's will, and their mutual recognition of this fact can prevent the party struggle from going bad without diminishing

---

[1] Reinhold Niebuhr, *Reflections on the End of an Era*, p. 14.

[2] J. H. Robinson, quoted by Karl Mannheim, *Freedom, Power and Democratic Planning*, p. 104.

[3] Quoted by E. H. Carr, *Conditions of Peace*, p. xxi.

147

its reality and even its bitterness. Like everything else, the recognition of the relativity of party divisions must not be carried too far. It was said of A. J. Balfour that 'his philosophic aloofness had induced in him the habit of mind, so dangerous in any politician, of being interested in both sides of a case'.[1] And it is never to be forgotten, as Dr Brunner has said, 'that God uses the genius of one-sidedness—which is perhaps a pleonasm—as much as the spirits of moderation'.[2]

(vi) Lastly, Z need not be constantly asking himself whether he is sufficiently different from other politicians or other citizens who do not profess the Christian faith. A Christian politician, like a Christian bus-driver, should be a normal practitioner of his own skill—doing all the things that a politician or a bus-driver ought to do as well as they can be done. What distinguishes the Christian is not that he necessarily does his job better than his comrades but that he knows the doing-well of his job glorifies God. He is thus in his prayers and worship able to serve as their priest, offering their work as well as his own to him who crowns all good work with his blessing.

Nevertheless, of course the question may fairly be asked, 'What difference does Christianity make?' and I cannot do better than to conclude this book with the answer to that question that was given by the same frontier group of Christian politicians in another document that it prepared for publication in *The Christian News-Letter*:

The statesman or politician who is also a Christian will, in the majority of decisions which he has to take, probably not act differently from one who makes no Christian profession. Nevertheless, however much he may be limited by the circumstances in which he has to act and by the public opinion which he represents and to which he is responsible, there should

[1] See Harold Nicolson, *King George V*, p. 90.
[2] E. Brunner, *Natural Theology*, p. 59. Quotations in the foregoing paragraphs, except where otherwise indicated, are from *C.N.L.*, No. 263 (26th June, 1946).

always be present in his mind three considerations which may at critical points profoundly influence what he decides to do.

First, he will be aware of the corrupting power of unconscious bias. He will realize how easy it is for national or class self-interest to masquerade under the guise of high-sounding principle or to twist the principle in its application, and he will be ceaselessly vigilant to make the effort of intellectual and spiritual self-examination necessary to ensure that he himself is not being misled.

In the second place, he will never be without a consciousness of the fallibility of his own judgment as a sinful man nor of the limitations of his foresight as a finite being. He will shrink, for example, from so black a deed as to launch a preventive war with weapons which involve the wholesale destruction of civilian populations, because he will be reluctant to regard as infallible the judgment that it is the only possible means of preserving the life of his nation. He will hesitate to take on his own shoulders a burden of responsibility that belongs to God alone.

But equally he will not recoil from difficult and costly decisions. He will resist the moral squeamishness which is unable to make a decision because of the gravity of the consequences. He knows that he has been placed where he is to act responsibly, and that after he has done his utmost to discover what is right, he has to put his conclusions fearlessly to the test of action, trusting the consequences to God and putting his hope in God's mercy and forgiveness. The man on whose decisions the lives and welfare of millions may depend cannot but know in experience more deeply than other men, that the only thing which makes it possible to act responsibly and unfalteringly in a world in which the consequences of our actions are hidden from us, and may turn out to be quite other than we intended, is a firm belief in the forgiving mercy and over-ruling providence of God.[1]

[1] *C.N.L.*, No. 277 (8th January, 1947).

Index of Names and Subjects

151

Index of References to Scripture